Children
Live Like
Jesus

Group
Loveland, Colorado

Helping Children Live Like Jesus
Copyright © 1997 Group Publishing, Inc.

Credits
Contributing Authors: Cindy Smith, Ken Kellner, and Liz Shockey
Editor: Jan Kershner
Senior Editor: Chris Yount
Managing Editor: Paul Woods
Chief Creative Officer: Joani Schultz
Copy Editor: Helen Turnbull
Art Director: Lisa Chandler
Cover Art Director: Helen H. Lannis
Computer Graphic Artist: Kari K. Monson
Cover Designer: Liz Howe
Cover Illustrator: Liz Howe
Illustrator: Shelley Dieterichs
Production Manager: Ann Marie Gordon

Unless otherwise noted, Scriptures quoted from The Youth Bible, New Century Version, copyright © 1991 by Word Publishing, Dallas, Texas 75039. Used by permission.

Library of Congress Cataloging-in-Publication Data

Smith, Cindy, 1957-
    Helping children live like Jesus / [contributing authors, Cindy Smith, Ken Kellner, and Liz Shockey].
       p.   cm.
    Summary: A collection of Bible lessons based on the life of Jesus.
    ISBN 1-55945-681-7
    1. Jesus Christ--Biography--Juvenile literature. 2. Christian education of children. [1. Jesus Christ--Biography. 2. Bible stories--N.T.] I. Kellner, Ken. II. Shockey, Liz. III. Title.
    BT302.S558 1997
    232.9'01--dc21
    [B]   96-6809
                                          CIP
                                          AC

ISBN 1-55945-681-7
Printed in the United States of America.
10 9 8 7 6 5 4 3 2   02 01 00 99 98 97

contents

introduction

Jesus is the cornerstone of our faith. And nothing is more important than helping children develop a deep, lasting relationship with him. But how can we accomplish this task?

By helping kids know Jesus better. In *Helping Children Live Like Jesus,* children will experience thirteen lessons from the Bible—right from the Gospels about the life of Jesus. Your children will learn about Jesus' life, his leadership, and his love. Only by knowing Jesus can kids ever hope to live like Jesus.

Jesus' life will become real to your kids as they learn biblical truths the active way. No more sitting still as someone reads the story from the front of the room. In *Helping Children Live Like Jesus,* you'll find activities that appeal to every learning style. Watch your kids' enthusiasm as they participate in crafts, skits, art projects, interactive stories, object lessons, and group dialogue. And prepare to be astounded at how much they actually retain from each lesson.

Each chapter begins with the Good News—a Bible-based focus for the lesson. You'll also find a quick lesson outline in "A Look at the Lesson" and a "Preparation" section listing simple supplies to have on hand. Many lessons contain photocopiable handouts. Depending on which activities you choose and the size of your class, your class time can be as flexible as your needs.

And *Helping Children Live Like Jesus* will teach kids how to apply what they've learned about Jesus to their daily lives. Have fun as you help your kids know, follow, and live like Jesus.

The Promise of a Savior

Scripture:
Matthew 1:20-23;
Luke 1:26-56

Good News:
God always keeps his promises.

God sent an angel to Joseph and Mary to announce the promise of his Son. You can imagine the questions that must have entered their minds: "How can this be?" "Why us?" "What will people say?" But God's messenger dispelled their doubts, telling them not to be afraid and promising that Mary's baby would be the Son of God. Scripture tells us that Joseph and Mary believed the angel's promise, humbly trusting God's will for their lives.

We can instill that same trust in young children. One way to do that is by helping kids discover God's faithfulness to his Word. The many promises found throughout the Bible are ours to receive, believe, and enjoy. Sometimes there may be a waiting period before the fulfillment of a promise, just as Mary waited for the birth of Jesus. But God is always faithful, and he always keeps his promises.

Use this lesson to encourage your students to trust in God and rely on his promises.

a look at the lesson

1. **DECORATION STATIONS** *(10 minutes)*
   Kids will prepare for a party and discuss why good things are worth waiting for.

2. **BROKEN PROMISES** *(10 minutes)*
   Students will have a relay race and discuss the importance of keeping promises.

3. **ACTION!** *(15 minutes)*
   Kids will make the Bible story from Luke 1:26-56 and Matthew 1:18-23 come alive by presenting a live mural.

4. **PROMISES, PROMISES** *(10 minutes)*
   Students will look up verses containing promises and present them in picture form.

5. **I BELIEVE!** *(10 minutes)*
   Kids will play Tag with a twist, and hear John 3:16 for the greatest promise of all.

6. **PROMISE PARTY** *(5 minutes)*
   Students will have a party to celebrate God's faithfulness.

preparation

Gather Bibles, poster board, markers, tape, balloons, crepe paper, construction paper, scissors, toothpicks, masking tape, paper, pencils, newsprint, index cards, colored pencils, newspaper, instant pudding and milk, a clean jar with a tight-fitting lid, a measuring cup, a pitcher, powdered drink mix and water, napkins, cookies, a bowl, paper plates, and plastic cups and spoons.

DECORATION STATIONS 1.

You'll need poster board, markers, newsprint, tape, balloons, crepe paper, construction paper, scissors, paper plates, napkins, cups, and spoons.

Say: I have good news and bad news. The good news is that we're going to have a party today. The bad news is that we have to wait until later. As we wait, let's decorate the room to make our party more fun. It's time to choose a Decoration Station!

Have kids form three groups to help decorate the room for the class party. Assign each group one of the following Decoration Stations:

● **Banner Boosters**—Provide a large sheet of poster board and markers. Have kids write: PROMISES, PROMISES, PROMISES . . . GOD ALWAYS KEEPS HIS! Suggest that kids decorate the banner with a giant rainbow to represent one of God's greatest promises. Tape the finished banner to a wall near your party table.

● **Table Toppers**—Have kids use newsprint to cover a party table. Have kids use markers to draw colorful designs on the "tablecloth."

Encourage kids to tear construction paper into small pieces to use as confetti. Kids can scatter confetti on the party table after they set the table with paper plates, napkins, cups, and spoons.

● **Steady Streamers**—Have kids blow up and tie off balloons of different colors. Have kids hang the balloons and crepe paper streamers around the party table.

When all of the Decoration Stations are complete, gather everyone together and say: **Everything looks great for our party. Now all we have to do is wait!** Ask:

● **What's it like to have to wait for good things?**

● **What things are hard for you to wait for?**

Say: **Good things are worth waiting for. Every year we look forward to Christmas, birthdays, and other holidays. God's promises are a lot like holidays. We may have to wait, but God always keeps his promises.**

People, however, sometimes break their promises, don't they? Let's see what that's like.

2. BROKEN PROMISES

Form two groups, and have groups line up at one end of the room. On a table at the other end of the room, set out half of the toothpicks and a roll of masking tape for each group.

> You'll need one toothpick for every two students and two rolls of masking tape.

Say: **Let's have a relay race. The first person in each line will hop to the table, break a toothpick in two, and hop back to the line. The next person in line will hop to the table, tape the toothpick back together, and hop back to the line. Try to tape the toothpick back together exactly as it was before it was broken. Then continue until everyone has either broken or taped together a toothpick. Ready? Go!**

When all of the toothpicks have been taped back together, have kids sit in a circle. Set the mended toothpicks in the center. Ask:

● **What was it like to tape the toothpicks back together?**

● **Are the toothpicks as strong as they were before they were broken? Explain.**

● **How are mended toothpicks like broken promises?**

● **How does it feel when someone breaks a promise to you?**

● **How do broken promises affect a relationship?**

Say: **In our race, it was hard to tape the toothpicks back together exactly as they were before they were broken. Just as it was hard to mend the toothpicks, sometimes it's hard to mend a relationship after someone breaks a promise. We never have to worry about broken promises with God, because God always keeps his promises. Let's look in the Bible for one of God's promises.**

You'll need Bibles, newsprint, markers, scissors, paper, and pencils.

Form three groups and assign each group one of the following passages: Luke 1:26-38; Luke 1:39-56; or Matthew 1:18-23. Give each group a large piece of newsprint, markers, and scissors.

Say: **In your group take turns reading the verses from your Bible passage. Then use the markers to turn your paper into the background for a live mural of your story. Draw the background and bodies of the people involved in your story. Then cut out holes for the head and arms. The kids playing the characters in your story will put their heads and arms through the holes and "act out" the story for the rest of the class.**

Think of a short dialogue for your characters to say as they present what happened in the Bible passage. Choose someone in your group to be the narrator who'll set the stage for your story. Those who don't have speaking parts will help hold the ends of the mural.

Provide paper and pencils for kids to create a script for the narrator to work from. Circulate among the groups and offer help and suggestions as needed. For example, Group 1 will need a narrator, Mary, and Gabriel. Group 2 will need a narrator, Mary, and Elizabeth. Group 3 will need a narrator, Joseph, and an angel.

Encourage the kids to use as much facial, arm, and hand motions as possible.

Have groups display their live murals and present their dramas. Give each group a rousing round of applause. Then ask:

● **What was the message the angel brought to Mary and Joseph?**

● **Think of a time you were given very important news. Were you surprised? Did you believe the news?**

Ask a child to read aloud Luke 1:45, then ask:

● **What did Mary have to do to receive God's promise?**

Say: **When God promises something, we can believe it! God always keeps his promises. Let's look in the Bible for more of God's promises.**

4. PROMISES, PROMISES

Before class, write each of the following Scripture references on a separate index card: Genesis 9:11; Psalm 136:1; Matthew 11:28; Luke 11:9; and John 14:2. You'll need one card for every two students in your class. It's OK to repeat the Scripture reference on different cards.

You'll need Bibles, colored pencils, index cards, and tape.

Form pairs and give each pair one of the Scripture cards. Supply colored pencils for kids to use.

Say: **Look up your Scripture reference to discover God's promise contained in the verse. Then, on the other side of your card, use colored pencils to write the promise or part of the promise in a shape that represents that promise. For instance, Psalm 136:1 has a promise that God's love will continue forever. So you could write the words "God's love continues forever" in the shape of a heart. Repeat the words as many times as necessary to complete your shape. Include the reference—or where to find the verse in the Bible—somewhere in the shape.**

When kids have finished their drawings, have them each display and explain their finished product. Then have kids tape their cards to the banner they made in the "Decoration Stations" activity. Ask:

- **Which of these promises means the most to you? Why?**
- **Why do you think God puts promises in his Word?**
- **How do you feel when you see God's promises in the Bible? Why?**

Say: **God's Word is full of precious promises. We can have peace and joy, because we can always count on God. Now let's play a game to remind us of God's greatest promise of all.**

5. I BELIEVE!

Have kids help you wad up several sheets of newspaper. Then say: **Let's play I Believe Tag. I'll choose one person to be "It." It will stand in the middle of the room with a pile of these paper "faith killers." Faith killers are things that keep people from believing God's promises.** Ask:

You'll need Bibles and newspaper.

- **What could some faith killers be?** (Kids may answer fear, doubt, unbelief, or people telling you not to believe.)

Say: **In this game, the rest of you will try to get to the opposite wall without being hit by the faith killers. We'll call the opposite wall "heaven." If you're hit by a faith killer, you have to freeze in that position until you say "I believe!"**

After the first round of play, choose a new It, and have kids help pick up the paper wads. Play a few more rounds, then have kids sit in a circle. Ask:

- **What was it like trying to get across the room without being** hit by the faith killers?

● Is it possible to get to heaven without believing God's promises? Explain.

Say: **We all have things that test our faith. But these tests don't have to keep us from getting to heaven. The Bible gives us God's promise for us to get to heaven. Let's see what that promise is.**

Have a child read aloud John 3:16. Then ask:

● What was the only way to make sure you made it to the other wall?

● According to this verse, what is the only way to make sure you'll get to heaven?

Say: **That's right. If we believe that Jesus is God's Son, and if we have faith in him, we'll go to heaven. That's the greatest promise of all! Mary believed God's promise that Jesus would be the Son of God, and we can believe God's promise for eternal life. Isn't it great that God always keeps his promises? Let's celebrate with a Promise Party!**

PROMISE PARTY 6.

You'll need napkins, pre-sweetened powdered drink mix and water, a pitcher, instant pudding and cold milk, a measuring cup, a clean jar with a tight-fitting lid, cookies, and plastic cups and spoons.

Say: Well, you had to wait a little while, but I told you we'd have a party today. You can help me make the snack. Form three groups: the Shakers, the Crumblers, and the Mixers. The Shakers make Promise Pudding by combining the instant pudding and milk in the jar, then take turns shaking the contents until the pudding thickens. Then they pour the pudding into individual cups.

The Crumblers make You Can Believe Crunch by crumbling the cookies into a large bowl to use as topping for the pudding. The Mixers prepare Promise Punch by mixing the powdered drink mix and water. Have kids set out all the finished snacks on the party table decorated in the first activity.

Before enjoying the snack, ask:

● How did it feel to have to wait for the promise of a party?

● What does the promise of God's gift of eternal life through Jesus mean to you?

● What is it like knowing that God always keeps his promises?

Say: **Before we enjoy our snack, let's thank God for the sweetness of his promises.**

Pray: **Dear God, thank you for always keeping your promises. Thank you, especially, for sending us Jesus. We believe your promise that if we believe in him, we'll go to heaven. In Jesus' name, amen.**

Jesus Is Born!

Good News:
We can tell others
the good news
about Jesus.

Year after year, from the time we were children, most of us have heard the familiar Christmas story. So the shepherds who visited baby Jesus on that first Christmas are almost like our old friends. There they were, tending their sheep and taking care of business as usual, when the angel of the Lord appeared to them and delivered a message so extraordinary, so thrilling, that they immediately left their sheep and ran to see this thing that happened. God didn't choose a prophet or a priest or a king to be the first to hear this good news—he entrusted the message to the humble, ordinary people.

We can teach children to recognize that the responsibility and joy of sharing the good news is not just for an elite few. Every child of God, no matter the age or occupation, has been commissioned to go into all the world and preach the Gospel.

Use this lesson to bring greater understanding of the good news and awaken a desire in your young children to share that news.

a look at the lesson

1. **A WELCOME INTERRUPTION** *(5 minutes)*
Kids will be interrupted to help them identify with the shepherds' angelic interruption.

2. **LET ME TELL YOU** *(10 minutes)*
Kids will share their good news in a creative way.

3. **GOOD NEWS!** *(13 minutes)*
Students will listen to the Bible story from Luke 2:1-20 and relay objects to their classmates, just as good news is passed to others.

4. **DON'T HOLD BACK** *(12 minutes)*
Students will try to get an important message to another classmate and discuss hindrances to sharing the Gospel.

5. **IT'S A BOY!** *(10 minutes)*
Kids will create birth announcements for Jesus' birth to be given away to friends outside of class.

6. **MORE AND MORE** *(10 minutes)*
Kids will read Psalm 34:8 and discuss how one "taste" of God will cause a hunger for more of God.

preparation

Gather construction paper, a bowl of trail mix, paper cups, a towel, a container, a varied assortment of candies and fruits, Bibles, paper, pencils, scissors, markers or crayons, glue sticks, plastic spoons, graham crackers with icing, a cassette or CD with "Silent Night" and a cassette or CD player. You'll also need the cutouts from the "Spread the News" handout (p. 17), one small blanket, and one picture of an angel.

A WELCOME INTERRUPTION

You'll need construction paper, a large bowl of trail mix, a towel, and a container such as a bowl or box. Before class, hide a bowl of trail mix under a towel in a secluded corner of your room.

In an area of your room away from the bowl of trail mix, have kids tear confetti-sized pieces of construction paper and place them in the empty container. After a few minutes, lift the corner of the covered snack and peek underneath.

Say: **Wow! Look at this! This is wonderful! This looks great!**

After kids voluntarily come over to see what you're talking about, remove the cover completely. Have kids sit in a circle and pass the trail mix around for kids to eat as you ask the following questions. Ask:

● Why did you stop what you were doing?

● What kind of good news might make you stop right in the middle of an important task?

● What are some ways people spread news?

Say: Today we're going to hear about shepherds who stopped what they were doing when angels surprised them with very good news. Let's talk more about spreading good news.

Save the confetti for use in a later activity.

2. LET ME TELL YOU

Say: Think of some good news you'd like to share with your classmates. It might be that you got a new pet or that your grandparents are coming to visit. Keep the news a secret until it's time to reveal it.

You'll need no supplies.

Give kids a few moments to think of good news to spread, then have kids sit in a circle on the floor.

Say: Take turns sharing the good news you thought of in a creative way. For instance, you may whisper it to the person sitting next to you, and then that person will whisper it to the next, and so on around the circle. Or another example would be to pantomime the news, or tell it by playing Charades. Use your imagination to share your good news with the rest of the class.

After children have revealed their good news, ask:

● How did it feel to have to wait to share your good news?

● What was it like to share your good news with your classmates?

● What was it like to receive good news from your classmates?

Say: It's fun to tell others good news, and it's fun to receive good news. In our Bible story today, we'll learn how God sent a special messenger from heaven to spread good news. Let's find out what this good news was.

TEACHER TIP

If you have more than eight students in your class, form two groups for this activity.

3. GOOD NEWS!

Form pairs and have kids form a semicircle, with partners sitting beside each other in the semicircle.

Say: As I tell our Bible story, listen very carefully. I'll stop after certain sentences that contain clues. Each time I stop, I'll motion to a different pair to hurry up to the table and try to figure out which object on the table represents the clue in the sentence. Show me the object you've chosen and I'll nod whether it's correct or not. If it's correct, put it back on the table and sit down again. If it's not correct,

You'll need a photocopy of the "Spread the News" handout (p. 17), a picture of an angel, and a small blanket. Before this activity, put the following objects on a table in your room: the cutouts from the "Spread the News" handout, a picture of an

choose again. Are you ready?

Read the following story, pausing at the italicized cue words to let pairs come forward to choose an object. Emphasize the italicized words in the story, but do not read aloud the words in parentheses.

Augustus Caesar was *ruler* over Rome. *(Crown)*

He ordered everyone to travel to the towns they were born in and sign their names on a list. So Joseph took Mary, who was pregnant, left Nazareth, and *traveled* to Bethlehem. *(Map)*

Bethlehem was very crowded, and there were *no rooms* left in the inns where they wanted to stay. *("NO VACANCY" sign)*

Joseph and Mary found a place to stay in a stable for animals. While they were there, Mary gave birth to her first son. Mary wrapped him in a *blanket* and placed him in a manger, or straw bed. *(Blanket)*

That night, some shepherds were in a nearby field guarding their flocks of *sheep*. *(Sheep)*

Suddenly, an angel appeared, and the hills were *lit up* with the glory of God. *(Flashlight)*

The angel encouraged the shepherds not to be afraid. The angel told the shepherds he was bringing good news of a Savior who had just been born in Bethlehem and explained they would find the Savior lying in a *manger*. *(Manger)*

Suddenly, the *angel* was joined by a great crowd of other *angels* and they all began praising God and singing glory to God in heaven. *(Picture of an angel)*

When the angels left, the shepherds hurried to Bethlehem. They found Mary and Joseph and saw the baby lying in the manger. The shepherds *announced* to everyone what the angel had said about the child. *(Megaphone)*

Then the shepherds returned to their flocks thanking God for all they had seen and heard.

After the story, say: **You all did a great job of figuring out the clues in this story!**

Ask:

● **Why do you think God used angels to proclaim the birth of Jesus?**

● **Why do you think God chose shepherds instead of kings to be the very first to hear about Jesus?**

● **What did the shepherds do after they heard the good news?**

● **What's the first thing you do when you hear good news?**

Say: **It's exciting to hear good news. When we hear good news it's hard to keep it to ourselves. People had been waiting a long time for God's Son. They knew from the Scriptures in the Old Testament that a Savior would come who'd save his people. So when the angel announced the birth of this Savior, the shepherds were so excited that they ran to town and began telling others what they'd seen and heard.**

We can tell others the good news of Jesus too. Let's play a game about spreading news.

4. DON'T HOLD BACK

Say: Let's play a fun game where it's hard to spread news.

You'll need Bibles, paper, and pencils.

Have kids form a circle with one Listener inside the circle and three Tellers outside the circle. The kids who form the circle will be the Blockers. Give each of the Tellers a scrap of paper and a pencil, and explain that the Tellers are to write on the paper a message they'd like to give to the Listener.

Say: **Tellers, you'll try to spread your news to the Listener inside the circle. Blockers, you'll try to keep the Tellers from spreading their news. Ready? Go!**

Call time when the Tellers have managed to tell their news to the Listener or when it becomes apparent that they'll be unable to accomplish that goal. If you have time, play another round with new volunteers. After the game, ask:

- **Tellers, what was it like trying to spread your news?**
- **What obstacles did you have to overcome to spread your news?**
- **What things helped you deliver your news?**
- **How was our game like trying to spread the good news about Jesus?**

Ask a child to read aloud Mark 16:15.

Say: **The Bible tells us to tell others about Jesus, but sometimes that may seem hard to do.**

Ask:

- **What kinds of things block us from telling the good news of Jesus?**
- **When is it hard for you to tell others about Jesus?**
- **Who would you like to tell about Jesus this week? What would you like to tell them about Jesus?**

Say: **God can help us tell the good news about Jesus.** The shepherds in our Bible story were excited to tell others about baby Jesus. In this next activity, we'll be telling about baby Jesus, too.

5. IT'S A BOY!

Say: When a baby is born, many parents send out birth announcements to tell people all about the baby. Let's make birth announcements for Jesus' birth. You may want to draw a picture of what you think the manger scene looked like. You can add whatever information you think people need to know about Jesus. Also add a statement about why Jesus came to earth. It might help to look back at our Bible story in Luke 2 to find what the angels said about Jesus.

You'll need Bibles, construction paper, scissors, markers or crayons, glue sticks, and confetti from the first activity.

Give each child a sheet of construction paper. Supply Bibles, colored markers, glue sticks, and the confetti from the first activity. Give kids several minutes to write and decorate their announcements, then invite them to show their creations.

Have a child read aloud Isaiah 40:9. Ask:

● **When this verse says to "shout," it doesn't necessarily mean to go outside and yell at the top of your voice. What do you think "shout" means in this verse?**

● **How can we communicate the good news of Jesus?**

● **Who first told you about Jesus? What did this person say?**

Say: **There are many ways to spread the good news of Jesus. This week, give your birth announcement to someone who needs to hear about Jesus. Be ready to tell about your experience at the beginning of class next week.**

MORE AND MORE **6.**

You'll need Bibles (either New International or King James Versions), graham crackers with icing, a cassette or CD with "Silent Night," and a cassette or CD player.

Have kids sit in a circle. Give each child a bite-sized piece of a graham cracker with icing. Set out the rest of the snack in full view of the children. Ask:

● **How does your graham cracker taste?**

● **Does this one bite satisfy you so you don't want any more? Explain.**

Say: **Let's read aloud Psalm 34:8 together.**

Have kids read the verse together. Then ask:

● **What do you think this verse means?**

● **When we get a "taste" of God, or are introduced to him, why do you think we hunger for more of him?**

Say: **When we tell others about Jesus, they get a taste of the goodness of God. Many of the people we tell about Jesus will want to know more about him. The more we taste of Jesus' goodness, the more we'll want to know.**

Softly play "Silent Night." Have kids hold hands. Say: **Let's say a circle prayer to thank God for the privilege of sharing the good news about Jesus. I'll begin by saying one thing about Jesus. Then we'll go around the circle to the right, and each of you can add what you'd like to say about Jesus.**

When everyone in the circle has spoken, end the prayer by saying: **Thank you, God, for your wonderful Son. Help us share the good news about Jesus every day. In Jesus' name, amen.**

Hand out the rest of the graham crackers and end your class with a time of fellowship where kids can interact with each other.

Spread the News

Jesus Grows Up

Scripture:
Luke 2:41-52

Good News:
We can learn about God.

Very little is written in the Bible about Jesus as a boy. But God included exactly what he wanted us to know. The trip to Jerusalem when Jesus was twelve years old reveals the young boy's love and zeal for his heavenly Father. We see in this passage his great desire to be in a place where people were learning and growing in the knowledge of God. And we see the wisdom Jesus exhibited as he amazed the Temple priests with his knowledge about God. Jesus was obedient to his parents; he grew in wisdom (mentally), in stature (physically), and in favor with God (spiritually) and man (socially).

Jesus is always our example. We often look only at his life as an adult, but his example as a child shows that we should continually seek to know about God. By the time kids reach third grade, many have developed interests and acquired knowledge about the things they're passionate about. But they may perceive that the things of God are difficult to understand and therefore only for adults.

Use this lesson to stir up their desire to know God. By looking at Jesus' example, your students will learn that God wants them to learn and grow in the knowledge of him.

a look at the lesson

1. **PERFECT PRAISE** *(8 minutes)*
   Kids will experience a balancing relay and discuss how practice improves skill.

2. **QUESTION MARKS** *(8 minutes)*
   Kids will play a yes-or-no question game to understand the importance of asking questions to learn.

3. **PICTURE STORY** *(12 minutes)*
   Students will draw pictures while they listen to the Bible story from Luke 2:41-52.

4. **GROW AND KNOW** *(13 minutes)*
   Kids will practice ways to learn about God and will discuss James 1:25.

5. **LET'S TALK** *(10 minutes)*
   Students will learn more about their classmates, and read various Scriptures to see the value of prayer.

6. **GROWING UP IN GOD** *(10 minutes)*
   Kids will compare what's necessary for seeds to grow with what's necessary for them to grow in God.

preparation

Gather Bibles, two hard-backed books, paper, markers, recent newspapers, the "Grow and Know" handout (p. 25), flower seeds, spoons, paper cups, potting soil, and a watering can.

PERFECT PRAISE 1.

You'll need two hard-back books.

Form two teams. Have each team line up on the same side of your room. Give the first person in each line a hardback book.

Say: **We're going to have a balancing relay. Balance the book on your head, quickly walk to the other end of the room, touch the wall, and return to your team. Give the book to the second person in line who'll do the same thing. Continue this process until everyone has run the relay. If you drop the book at any time, you must begin again. Ready? Go!**

After the relay, ask:

- **Was this activity easy or hard? Why?**
- **What would make this activity easier?**
- **How important is it to practice when you learn a new skill?**
- **Do you think it's ever possible to be really good at something without practicing? Explain.**
- **What are some things you've learned to do well by practicing?**

Say: Many of the things you mentioned you learned to do well at school. School is a good place to practice skills such as math and spelling. Church is a good place to learn and practice, too. Let's talk about how we can practice learning about God.

2. QUESTION MARKS

Have kids sit in a circle. Ask:

● **What are different ways we learn things?**

You'll need no supplies.

Say: **We can learn a lot just by asking questions. Let's play a quick game by asking questions.**

Select one child to think of an object in the room. Have the other kids ask yes-and-no questions to try to identify that object. For example, the kids could begin by asking, "Is this object to your right?" "Is this object smaller than your hand?" "Is this object red?" Play the game with several volunteers, then ask:

● **Why is it important to ask questions when we're trying to learn something new?**

● **What questions do you have about God?**

● **What questions would you like to ask God?**

Say: **Those are all really good questions. We learn about things when we ask questions. God wants us to learn and grow by listening and asking questions. When Jesus was a boy, he listened and asked questions, too.**

3. PICTURE STORY

Give each child a sheet of paper and a marker. Say: **Listen as I tell the Bible story. I'll stop every once in a while to give you time to draw pictures during the story. You'll have to draw as quickly as you can to be ready for the rest of the story.**

You'll need paper and markers.

Say: **Our story comes from Luke 2:41-52.** Open your Bible to Luke 2:41-52 and show kids the chapter.

Then tell the following story: **At a certain time each year, all the Jewish people gathered in Jerusalem for Passover. Passover is a celebration of singing, dancing, and feasting to thank God for protecting the Jewish people when they were freed from slavery.**

When Jesus was twelve years old, he and his family traveled to Jerusalem as usual to celebrate the yearly Passover. There was a large group of people because many of Jesus' relatives and neighbors traveled with them.

Ask:

● **When you take vacations, what kinds of things do you do to** make the time pass more quickly?

Jesus' family probably did exactly as we do when we take long trips—played games, sang songs, and ate packed lunches from home. But since there were no cars, they spent many days walking.

Say: **Draw a picture of Jesus' family traveling.** Give kids a moment to draw, then continue: **When they finally arrived in Jerusalem, they celebrated with lots of good food, worshiped God in the Temple, and spent time with old friends. When the feast was over, Jesus' family and friends began the long journey home. After traveling all day, Mary and Joseph looked for Jesus. It was getting dark, and Mary and Joseph probably wanted to make sure Jesus got a good night's sleep. They thought he had been traveling with other family members, but when they looked for him, he was nowhere to be found!**

Ask:

● **What do you think your parents would do if they couldn't find you?**

● **How do you think Mary and Joseph felt when they couldn't find Jesus?**

Say: **Draw a picture of Mary and Joseph looking for Jesus.** Give kids a moment to draw, then continue: **Mary and Joseph hurried back to Jerusalem as fast as they could. They hunted for Jesus for three days before they finally found him.**

Ask:

● **Where do you think Jesus' parents found him?**

Say: **Draw a picture of where you think Jesus was.** Give kids a moment to draw, then continue.

Mary and Joseph found Jesus in the Temple, listening to the teachers and asking them many questions. Everyone who heard Jesus was surprised at how much he knew about God and at the answers he gave. His parents were amazed too. They said, "Jesus, we've been worried about you. We couldn't find you anywhere."

Jesus replied, "You shouldn't have had to look so hard. You should have known I would have been here in the Temple, in my Father's house."

Ask:

● **Why do you think Jesus chose to go to the Temple?**

Say: **Draw a picture of Jesus in the Temple.** Give kids a moment to draw, then continue:

Jesus returned home with his parents and obeyed them. Jesus learned more and more, and God was very pleased with him.

Give kids time to share and explain their drawings. Then ask:

● **Where do you go when you have questions about God?**

● **How can Jesus be an example to us in this story?**

Say: **We can learn about God by spending time in church. It's important to go to church, listen, and ask questions so we can learn more about God.**

4. GROW AND KNOW

Form pairs. Give each pair a copy of the "Grow and Know" handout. Say: **With your partner, follow the directions in each box on your paper. Be prepared to tell your insights to the rest of the class.**

Give children time to follow the directions on the handout. Then have children share insights they gained from this activity. Ask:

You'll need a Bible, recent newspapers, and a copy of the "Grow and Know" handout (p. 25) for every two students in your class.

● **What do you think Jesus would do about the problem you read in the newspaper?**

● **What's one thing you've learned about God this week?**

Say: **We can learn about God every day. The Bible says that learning about God will make us happy.**

Have a child read aloud James 1:25. Then ask:

● **Why do you think learning about God makes us happy?**

● **What's one way you can learn more about God this week?**

Say: **We can learn about God every day. Right now, let's learn more about each other.**

5. LET'S TALK

Form groups of four. Explain that children will have two minutes to find out as much as they can about the other people in their group. They might want to ask each other questions about favorite foods, pets, or sports.

You'll need Bibles.

After two minutes, call time and have each person tell something he or she learned about another person. Then say: **When you make new friends, you often spend a lot of time talking with them to find out more about them.**

Ask:

● **What kinds of things do you talk about with your friends?**

● **What kinds of things do you think God wants you to talk to him about?**

● **Do you think God ever gets tired of listening to us? Explain.**

● **Do you think Jesus ever needed to pray? Why or why not?**

Ask volunteers to read aloud Mark 1:35, Mark 6:45-46, Luke 5:16, and Luke 6:12.

Ask:

● **Why do you think Jesus spent so much time in prayer?**

● **Why is it important for us to pray?**

Say: **Jesus needed to communicate with God. And he wants us to talk to God, too. When we spend time in prayer we can learn more about God.**

You'll need a Bible, a package of flower seeds, spoons, paper cups, potting soil, and a watering can. Before this activity, cover a work table with newspaper.

Give each student a paper cup, a spoon, and a few flower seeds. Have the kids partially fill their cups with potting soil. Then have them plant and lightly water their flower seeds.

Form a circle. Ask:

● **What do seeds need to grow into healthy, strong plants?**

● **What happens if the seeds don't receive enough water or sun?**

● **What do we need to grow in our knowledge of God?**

● **What might happen if we stop learning about God?**

Say: **We can learn more about God by following Jesus' example. We can go to church, we can ask questions, we can learn from the Bible, and we can pray.** Ask:

● **What's one thing you'll do this week to help you learn more about God?**

Have a child read Luke 2:52.

Say: **We can all learn more about God.**

Beginning with yourself, pass the Bible around the circle and have each person read Luke 2:52 aloud, replacing the name of Jesus with the name of the person sitting to their right. For example, you might say, "Natalie became wiser and grew physically. People liked her, and she pleased God."

Close with a prayer thanking God for loving us enough to want to communicate with us. Encourage kids to take their flower pots home to remind them that we can learn more about God.

Grow and Know

With a partner, follow the directions in each box below.

Start ▷

Box 1

Read a short newspaper article that describes a problem in your town or country. Talk with your partner about what Jesus might do or say in that situation.

Box 2

Think of a friend you'd like to tell about Jesus. Then ask your partner to pray that God will help you follow through.

Box 3

Tell your partner one way you'd like to grow in faith. Then pray together for God's help.

Box 4

Name something you've learned about God and Jesus this week.

Box 5

Tell about a time you knew God was with you. What did that teach you about God?

Finish ▷

Jesus Calls the Disciples

Scripture:
Matthew 4:18-22

Good News:
We can be followers of Jesus.

Jesus had a mission to accomplish when he came to earth. Luke 4:18 says he was anointed to preach the good news to the poor, announce freedom for prisoners, give sight to the blind, free everyone who suffers, and proclaim the free favors of the Lord. Jesus chose twelve disciples who would learn from him and carry on the task of spreading the kingdom of God.

Most of the disciples Jesus chose were not highly educated people, renowned speakers, or even extremely powerful men of their time. But Jesus changed their lives, and they changed the lives of others because they followed the Son of God.

Use this lesson to help your students realize that they, too, can follow in the footsteps of Jesus.

a look at the lesson

1. **THE DRAFT** *(10 minutes)*
   Kids will choose players from sports cards and discuss the reasons for their choices.

2. **FOLLOW MY LEAD** *(10 minutes)*
   Students will imitate each other as they read Matthew 4:18-22, then discuss the difficulties of following.

3. **FISHERS OF MEN** *(10 minutes)*
   Kids will create their own fishing lures using candy and learn what Jesus meant when he called his disciples to be "fishers of men."

4. **FOLLOW HIS LEAD** *(15 minutes)*
   Kids will read Scriptures, and decide how to follow Jesus in real-life situations.

5. **FOLLOWERS CLUB** *(10 minutes)*
   Students will use magazine pictures to depict Jesus' twelve disciples and create a "Jesus' Followers Club" poster.

6. **JOIN THE CLUB!** *(5 minutes)*
   Kids will add their names to the "Jesus' Followers Club" poster and talk about the instructions Jesus gives his followers.

preparation

Gather several packets of sports cards. (Sports cards may be purchased inexpensively in grocery or discount stores. Or look for used cards at flea markets or garage sales.) You'll also need Bibles, toothpicks, one photocopy of the "What Would You Do?" handout (p. 33) for every four students, pencils, paper, a paper sack, newsprint, markers, scissors, old magazines, and tape.

Also gather bags of small, soft candies such as miniature marshmallows, gummy bears, or spice drops.

THE DRAFT 1.

You'll need several packets of sports cards.

Form groups of three. Give each group an assortment of sports cards. Say: **From these sports cards, choose three players you'd like to have on your team if you owned a professional team.**

Give kids several minutes to evaluate and choose players for their teams. Ask:

● **What made you decide on these particular players?**

● **What are the major factors a team owner considers when choosing players?**

● **What qualities do you think Jesus would consider necessary** for players on his team?

Say: **Jesus chose disciples to be on his team, but it wasn't because of their great ability, wealth, or power. There is only one thing necessary to have to join Jesus' team—and that's faith. Today we're going to find out what it means to be a follower of Jesus.**

②. FOLLOW MY LEAD

Form pairs, and give each pair a Bible. Have pairs open their Bibles to Matthew 4:18-22.

You'll need Bibles.

Say: **We're going to play a form of Follow the Leader. In this game, you're going to imitate each other as you read verses 18 through 22. Decide which one of you will read the first three verses. That person will be the first Leader. The Follower must try to imitate the Leader in motions and voice. In other words, do what the Leader does and speak the way he or she speaks.**

The Leader will read the first three verses a phrase at a time using different voice inflections. For example, you could whisper "As Jesus was walking by Lake Galilee" and then sing "he saw two brothers, Simon (called Peter) and his brother Andrew." You could shout out the next phrase and squeak like a mouse on the following phrase. You could also act out the motions by walking in place and pretending to be great followers. The Follower will try to mimic the Leader as much as possible.

When you've finished the first three verses, switch roles and read the next two verses.

Give kids time to read the verses. Allow time for plenty of giggles! When kids have finished reading, have kids discuss the following questions with their partners. Allow time after each question for pairs to tell their responses to the rest of the class. Ask:

● **What was it like to follow your partner? Explain.**

● **What do you think it means to be a follower of someone or something?**

● **What do you think Jesus meant when he told these 12 men to follow him?**

● **How much time each day do you think Jesus' followers spent with him?**

● **How is it possible to be Jesus' follower today?**

Say: **Even though we can't see Jesus with our physical eyes, we can still follow him. Let's discover how each of us can help others be Jesus' followers today.**

FISHERS OF MEN 3.

You'll need fancy, long toothpicks; Bibles; and bags of small, soft candies, such as miniature marshmallows, gummy bears, or spice drops. Kids will be making candy fishing lures, so bring in a few actual fishing lures to use as examples if possible.

Set the bags of candy in the center of a table. Gather kids around the table, and give each child three toothpicks. Caution kids not to run or to poke others with the toothpicks. Ask:

● **Has anyone here ever been fishing?**

Say: **Four of Jesus' disciples were fishermen by trade—Andrew, Peter, James, and John. Fishermen often use lures to catch fish. A lure is an object that fishermen attach to the end of their fishing lines to attract fish. Use this candy to create your own fishing lures.**

Show kids how to make lures by threading several different types of small candies on a toothpick. When everyone is finished, have kids show their lures to the rest of the class. Compliment kids on their colorful creations, then ask:

● **What makes lures attractive to fish?** (They're colorful; sometimes they're shiny; fish think they're food.)

● **Name some things that would be important for someone to know who's beginning to learn how to catch fish.**

Say: **When Jesus asked Andrew, Peter, James, and John to follow him, they immediately left their fishing boats and nets behind and followed Jesus. Jesus told them he was going to teach them how to fish for people instead of fish. Let's read that verse.**

Have a child read aloud Matthew 4:19. Then ask:

● **What do you think Jesus meant when he told Peter and Andrew that he would teach them to fish for people?**

● **Name some things that would be important for someone to know who wants to catch people for God.**

Say: **We can be followers of Jesus. To do that, we need to learn all we can about Jesus so we can tell others. In our last lesson, we talked about ways we can learn more about God. Ask:**

● **What are ways we can learn more about God?**

Say: **Thanks for all your answers. When we have faith in Jesus, we can be his followers. Reading the Bible, going to church, praying, and telling others about Jesus are all things to do as Jesus' followers. Let's find out what else we can do as followers of Jesus.**

FOLLOW HIS LEAD 4.

You'll need photocopies of the "What Would You Do?" handout (p. 33), a paper sack, pencils, paper, and Bibles. Before class,

Form three groups, and give each group a sheet of paper and a pencil. Have each group choose a Picker, a Reader, a Recorder, and a Speaker. It's OK if kids have more than one role. If there are more than four students in each group, have the other kids act as Encouragers who involve everyone in the discussion.

The Picker will pick a slip from the paper sack, the Reader will read what's written on the slip, the Recorder will take notes of the group's discussion, and the Speaker will tell the group's insights to the rest of the class.

Allow a few moments for kids to choose their roles, then have the Pickers choose slips. Give the kids about three minutes to discuss their situations. Then call time.

Allow each group to have its Reader read the group's situation and its Speaker tell the group's decision. After the group finishes, have kids from other groups tell how they might've handled the same situation. Then have the Reader read the group's Bible passage to the class.

After all the groups have shared, have a child read aloud John 8:31. Ask:

● **According to this verse, what are the requirements of a follower or disciple of Jesus?**

● **Why does Jesus care about what we think, say, and do?**

● **How do our attitudes, words, and actions affect what others may think about Jesus?**

Say: **Those who follow Jesus imitate him. They try to do what he would do, say what he would say, and think what he would think. We can be followers of Jesus by following his example. Then others will see the goodness of God in us and want to become followers, too!**

> cut apart the sections of the "What Would You Do?" handout, and put the sections in a paper sack. You'll need one section for every four students in your class. It's OK to use the same situation for more than one group.

 5.

FOLLOWERS CLUB

At the top of a large sheet of newsprint write in large, bold letters:

Jesus' Followers Club

Rules: Imitate Jesus

Who Can Join: All those who believe in Jesus and want to follow him.

Job Description: To be fishers of men.

> You'll need newsprint, markers, scissors, old magazines, tape, and Bibles.

Then tape the newsprint to a wall.

Have kids form two groups and give each group old magazines, scissors, markers, tape, and Bibles. Have each group choose some group members to be Cutters, others to be Artists, and others to be Tapers.

Say: **Jesus chose twelve disciples, and he taught them about the kingdom of God so they could teach others. They were the first members of a club we're going to call "Jesus' Followers Club." Let's put up a picture gallery of these first club members.**

Have kids open their Bibles to Luke 6:14-16. Assign verse 14 to Group 1 and verses 15 and 16 to Group 2.

Say: **The Cutters in Group 1 will cut out magazines pictures to represent the six disciples found in verse 14. Cutters in Group 2 will cut out pictures to represent the six disciples listed in verses 15 and 16.**

The Artists can use the markers to add extra facial features such as beards and mustaches to the pictures. Then the Tapers can tape the pictures to the newsprint and write each disciple's name under his picture.

When all twelve pictures have been posted, gather kids around the newsprint. Ask:

● **What do you have in common with these men?**

Say: **These men left their jobs and their homes so they could follow Jesus. The Bible says the disciples who were fishing dropped their nets and left their boats to follow Jesus. They began to learn a new way of life.** Ask:

● **What do you do to show that you're Jesus' follower?**

Say: **There are certain things in our lives that we may need to drop and leave in order to follow Jesus. Lying, fighting, and disobeying are examples of those things.** Ask:

● **What is something you need to drop to be a better follower of Jesus?**

Say: **We can turn to the Bible to find out what Jesus wants us to do.**

JOIN THE CLUB! 6.

You'll need a marker, the "Jesus' Followers Club" poster from the "Follow His Lead" activity, and Bibles.

Gather the kids around the "Jesus' Followers Club" poster. Say: **Before Jesus went to heaven, he left specific instructions for his disciples. Let's find out what those instructions were.**

Form pairs, and give each pair a Bible. Have partners take turns reading the verses in Matthew 28:19-20. Then have them discuss the following questions. Allow time after each question for pairs to tell their insights to the rest of the class. Ask:

● **What can you do to help others follow Jesus?**

● **What do you think is the hardest part about being a follower of Jesus?**

● **What is one thing you can do this week as a follower of Jesus?**

Say: **Jesus gave us, his followers, a magnificent promise. He said he would never leave us. Let's take turns writing our names on this poster. As you write your name, say, "Thank you, Jesus, for choosing me to be one of your followers." I'll start.**

Begin by writing your name on the poster as you say the sentence prayer. Then pass the marker to the student next to you. After all students have written their names on the poster, say: **Let's keep this poster hanging in our classroom to remind us that we can all be followers of Jesus! As you go out this week to help others become followers, remember that Jesus promised to be with you.**

What Would You Do?

Situation 1

The kids in your neighborhood want to start a "Kool Kids Klub." The self-appointed leader gives you the names of kids who can join the club. You notice that the names of your two neighbors aren't on the list. When you mention this, the leader says, "We only want *cool* kids in our club!"

What would you say?

What would Jesus say? (Check out Matthew 7:12 for the answer!)

Situation 2

During summer break, your parents give you and your sister extra chores to do around the house. You have permission to go to a slumber party at a friend's house if you get all your work done. The day of the party, you go swimming and forget to do your chores. When you get home, you see your sister did your jobs for you. Your parents praise your hard work and send your sister to her room for not finishing her jobs. You know if you tell the truth, you won't be allowed to go to the party.

What would you do?

What would Jesus do? (Look up Ephesians 4:25 for a clue!)

Situation 3

Every day at school, you say a silent prayer before you eat lunch. Lately, a bunch of kids have been laughing at you and making fun of you for praying. At first you just ignored them, but it's really starting to bother you. You don't know if they've heard about God or not.

What would you do?

What would Jesus do? (Read Luke 12:8-9 and find out!)

Jesus Calms the Storm

Scripture:
Mark 4:35-41

Good News:
We can always depend on Jesus.

Jesus was sleeping soundly. He had just finished a whirlwind speaking tour and had healed many sick and hurting people. After a full day of teaching on the crowded hills near the Sea of Galilee, Jesus and his followers got into their boat to cross the lake. Jesus took the opportunity to rest.

Suddenly, a powerful wind came up on the lake. Waves crashed over the little boat, filling it with water almost instantly. The disciples were terrified. They seemed to forget all of the incredible miracles they'd seen Jesus perform. Afraid of drowning, they woke Jesus, imploring him for help. Jesus stood and commanded the wind and the waves to be still. Then Jesus turned to his followers and asked, "Why are you so afraid? Do you still have no faith?"

Just like the disciples, when our lives get stormy, we tend to forget the times that Jesus has come through for us. This lesson will help kids rely on Jesus and will remind them that they can always depend on him.

a look at the lesson

1. **I DOUBT IT!** *(10 minutes)*
   Kids will tell hard-to-believe stories and discuss doubting.

2. **DOUBT BOUT** *(10 minutes)*
   Kids will "make" a storm to re-enact the story from Mark 4 of Jesus calming the storm.

3. **LIFEBOATS** *(15 minutes)*
   Students will make lifeboats and find out how Jesus can keep their lives balanced.

4. **WAKE UP, JESUS!** *(10 minutes)*
   Kids will play a fun Tag game to underscore how we can call on Jesus when we have fears and doubts.

5. **CRAZY AND CALM** *(10 minutes)*
   Students will play a game in which biblical passages help calm them.

6. **A PRAYER ON THE WIND** *(5 minutes)*
   Kids will make a new "prayer sail" for their lifeboats and silently send off their prayers to God.

preparation

Gather Bibles, pencils, spray bottles, partially-filled boxes of rice with lids, paper fans or an electric fan, cardboard boxes, dishpans, buckets or bowls, paper, colored pencils, toothpicks, two-inch plastic foam balls, a knife, gummy candies, scissors, a timer with a loud alarm, and staplers.

I DOUBT IT! 1.

You'll need no supplies.

Have kids sit in a circle. Say: **If I told you that I just finished talking on the phone with the president of the United States, you probably wouldn't believe it. You would doubt my story. Doubting means that you don't quite believe something you see or hear.**

Ask:

● **Who can tell about a time you doubted what someone said?**

Give kids a few moments to talk, then say: **I can understand why you'd doubt some of those stories. Sometimes it's hard to know what to believe and what to doubt. Let's play a game that'll help us decipher this doubting dilemma.**

Form three groups. Say: **Within your group, think of three hard-to-believe stories to tell the rest of the class. You might think of fantastic vacations you've taken, skills you have, awards you've received, or something someone in your family has done. But here's the catch.**

One of the stories has to be true! In a few minutes, we'll tell our stories and play the game I Doubt It!

Give the groups a few minutes to think of their stories, then have each group choose a Storyteller. Ask the first Storyteller to relate his or her group's three stories. After each story, let the class decide if they believe the story. If kids believe the story, have them cheer and give a thumbs up sign. If they doubt the story, have them yell, "I doubt it!" and give a thumbs down sign. After the class has voted on the three stories, have the Storyteller say which story is actually true. Repeat for the other groups.

Then ask:
- **Why did you doubt some of the stories you heard?**
- **Why is it hard to know whether something is true or not?**
- **What are ways you can test whether something is true?**

Say: Sometimes it's hard to know whether what someone is telling you is the truth or not. But it's easier to decide if you know that person really well, and if you know that person loves you and wouldn't lie to you. Today we're going to see that even the disciples were doubters sometimes. But they had no reason to doubt Jesus. We'll learn, just as the disciples did, that we can always depend on Jesus.

2. DOUBT BOUT

Open your Bible to Mark 4, and show kids the chapter. Say: **In the Gospel of Mark, chapter 4, there's a story of how Jesus not only calmed the disciples' doubts but also calmed the weather! Now you can be part of the story. I need some people to help with sound effects and some to play the roles of the disciples and Jesus.**

You'll need a Bible, spray bottles, a sheet of poster board, partially-filled boxes of rice with lids, paper fans or an electric fan, and an upturned classroom table.

Assign volunteers the roles of Jesus, the disciples, and the sound effects. Then practice these cues and responses, saying the cue and having kids respond appropriately.
- Thunder—Wave a sheet of poster board.
- Lightning—Flash room lights on and off.
- Waves—Spray water from spray bottles.
- Wind—Wave paper fans or turn on an electric fan (change speeds for gentle and strong winds).
- Rain—Tap fingernails against table tops, or pat thighs.
- Calm Seas—Slowly tilt boxes of rice back and forth.

Have the kids who play Jesus and the disciples sit in the upturned table "boat" and pantomime their character's actions during the story.

Read the following story with expression, emphasizing the italicized words as cues and pausing to let kids perform their roles.

Jesus lay sleeping in the little fishing boat. He was tired from speaking to huge crowds and from healing many people. The *disciples* rested nearby. They were excited about all they had learned from Jesus and all the miracles they had seen him do. They enjoyed the *calm seas* that night as they sailed across the Sea of Galilee. The gentle *wind* made the night perfect for sailing.

Suddenly, with no warning, a furious storm arose on the lake. The *lightning* flashed on the dark water, and the *thunder* rumbled. The *disciples* were startled and jumped up, pointing at the huge, dark clouds that blotted out the stars they'd enjoyed just minutes before. The *wind* blew fiercely into their faces, and the rain started to pour down.

The heavy *wind* whipped up the seas around them and the *waves* crashed over the boat. The *disciples* held on to the boat and each other, scared that they were going to drown. The *wind, rain, thunder,* and *lightning* became worse and worse as the *waves* pounded the little boat.

Finally, the *disciples* were so terrified that they made their way over to *Jesus* and shook him until he woke. They shouted, "Lord, save us! We're going to drown!"

Jesus said to his disciples, "Why are you afraid? You don't have enough faith." Then *Jesus* stood up in the middle of this great storm and said in a commanding voice, "Quiet! Be still!" At once, the *wind* died down, the *thunder* and *lightning* stopped, the *waves* disappeared and the sea became completely calm.

The *calm seas* comforted the *disciples,* and the gentle *wind* calmed their spirits. After what they had just gone through, they asked each other, "Who is this? Even the wind and the waves obey him!"

The disciples were beginning to understand that they could always depend on Jesus.

Have the kids put the props away and gather in a circle. Ask:

● **Have you ever been caught in a terrible storm? What was that like?**

● **What do you think Jesus wants us to do when we're afraid?**

● **Like the disciples, do you ever doubt that Jesus will take care of you?**

● **Can you think of times Jesus calmed your fears?**

Say: The disciples were afraid, even though Jesus was in the boat with them. They didn't seem to have much faith. But when they relied on Jesus, they saw amazing results. Jesus will be with us during all the stormy times in our lives. We can always depend on Jesus.

LIFEBOATS 3.

You'll need two-inch plastic foam balls cut in half—one half for each child, two toothpicks for each child, two gummy candies for each child, paper, scissors, colored

Say: Let's say that your life is like a boat. As long as a nice, steady breeze is pushing you along, you have smooth sailing. But what if things don't go your way? How will your "lifeboat" perform in a storm? Let's find out by making our own little lifeboats.

Give each student a plastic foam ball half, paper, three toothpicks, and scissors. Have each student cut a two-inch paper triangle to use as a sail. Distribute colored pencils, and say: **Write the word "doubts" on one side of your sail and the word "fears" on the other side. This sail will represent how your lifeboat can be pushed around by doubts and fears.**

pencils, and several dish-pans.

Have kids attach the sail to the toothpick "mast" by carefully weaving the toothpick in and out of the paper sail a few times. Then have them stick this toothpick "mast" slightly toward the front on the flat side of the plastic foam ball. Set out several dishpans of water.

Say: **Now we're going to set sail. Carefully put your lifeboats on the water, and see how they sail. No splashing or wind yet, please.**

Ask:

● **How does your lifeboat sail?**

● **Does it seem to have any direction? Explain.**

Say: **Now let's see how these lifeboats work when a storm of problems suddenly comes up. Use your breath, and blow hard on the sail of your lifeboat.**

After the boats capsize, have the kids pull them out of the water. Ask:

● **Why did your lifeboat capsize or turn over?**

● **What pushed your lifeboat over?**

Say: **Sometimes we feel like our lives are capsizing. We feel like we may not make it through the storm that surrounds us.**

Ask:

● **What things threaten to "capsize" or turn over your life?**

● **What do you think our lifeboats need to keep them from capsizing?**

Say: **We need something to give our lifeboats stability, something to keep them from capsizing. Let's try adding something called ballast. Ballast is anything heavy carried in a boat to give the boat stability.**

Have kids poke two gummy candies through their remaining toothpick and then attach it to the bottom of the boat.

Say: **Now try sailing your lifeboat again. Blow on the sail as hard as you can.**

Ask:

● **Why do you think your lifeboat stayed up when you blew on it?**

● **How do you think the ballast works?**

Say: **Ballast works by adding stability to a boat—ballast keeps the boat steady in the water and keeps the boat from turning over.**

● **How does Jesus give our lives stability in storms or hard times?**

Have kids remove their lifeboats from the water and save them for later use.

Say: **I'm glad to have Jesus as the steady ballast on my boat of life. I know that he can keep me from capsizing in a storm of doubt and fear. We can always depend on Jesus.**

WAKE UP, JESUS! 4.

You'll need a timer with a loud alarm such as an egg timer, small paper slips, and pencils.

Clear a space in the middle of your room. Set out the paper slips and pencils at one end of the room. Choose one child to be "Jesus," and have him or her pretend to sleep at the other end of the room.

Say: **Let's pretend that we're the disciples and Jesus is sleeping. Now is our chance to bring concerns, fears, and doubts to him. Everybody but the person playing the part of Jesus will gather around the table and grab a pencil. I'll set the timer and say "go." You'll write a fear or doubt that you have in your life and then set down your pencil. You'll run to Jesus and gently set your paper next to him. Then you'll run back to the table and fill out another slip.**

When the timer goes off, Jesus will wake up, tag the first person he can, and say, "Be still!" That person will then take the role of Jesus, and we'll play the game again. We'll see how many fears and doubts we can give to Jesus.

Play the game as many times as you wish, setting the timer for varying amounts of time. When finished, collect the paper slips and put them aside. (You may want to take a look at them after class just to get an idea of what your kids are thinking.) Gather the kids together, and ask:

● **Can you ever bring too many concerns to Jesus? Why or why not?**

● **Do you ever think Jesus is sleeping when you bring concerns to him in prayer?**

● **Why can Jesus understand our doubts and fears?**

● **How does it make you feel to know that Jesus cares about your doubts and fears?**

Say: **Jesus says in Matthew 28:20, "I will be with you always..." We don't have to wake him up to listen to our needs. He'll be there for us whenever we run into a storm. We can always depend on Jesus.**

CRAZY AND CALM 5.

You'll need a sheet of paper and a pencil.

Say: When we're scared or upset, we can find words in the Bible to guide us and calm us. God gave us the Bible to teach and help us. Let's find out how God's Word can help us.

Ask:

● **What kinds of things upset you?** Write kids' answers on a sheet of paper.

List about eight responses, then say: **Let's call these things "crazies." I have a list of verses from the Bible that are helpful in calming the crazies. I call them "calmers."**

Each time I read a crazy, wiggle a finger, leg, arm or your head. You must stay in one spot. I'm going to keep reading crazies until

you're really wiggling.

Then I'll read a calmer. Each time I read a calmer, stop wiggling one thing.

Read from your list of crazies until kids are wiggling all over. Then, one by one, read from this list of calmers:

"Do not worry about anything" (Philippians 4:6).

"You cannot add any time to your life by worrying about it" (Luke 12:25).

"The Lord is my shepherd, I have everything I need" (Psalm 23:1).

"Be careful. Be calm and don't worry" (Isaiah 7:4b).

"Trust the Lord with all your heart" (Proverbs 3:5a).

"The Lord makes everything go as he pleases" (Proverbs 16:4a).

"He heals the brokenhearted" (Psalm 147:3a).

"I will be with you always" (Matthew 28:20b).

After everybody has calmed down, have them sit in a circle. Ask:

● **How did the calmer verses make you feel?**

● **What can you do in real life when the crazies seem out to get you?**

Say: **When you're upset or afraid, try to find a quiet place to sit and read verses like the calmers we just heard. Just as Jesus calmed the storm, we can depend on him to calm our lives. Let's ask Jesus to guide us right now.**

6. A PRAYER ON THE WIND

> You'll need the boats from the "Lifeboats" activity, paper, colored pencils, and one toothpick per student.

Say: **Before, our lifeboats had sails that were driven by fears and doubts. Fortunately, our ballast kept the boats from capsizing in stormy seas. Jesus can be like ballast in our lives. He can keep us steady when life gets hard. Jesus wants us to bring our fears and doubts, as well as our praises and needs, to him through prayer.**

Cut out another sail for your lifeboat, and write on it a short prayer such as, "I can always depend on you." Exchange it with the old sail, and put your lifeboat back in the water. As you calmly blow your boat away, say your silent prayer. Then take your lifeboat out of the water, and take it home with you as a reminder that you can always depend on Jesus.

Jesus Raises Lazarus

Scripture:
John 11:1-45

Good News:
Jesus gives us new life.

Jesus had many friends, just as we all do. Three of Jesus' special friends were Mary, Martha, and Lazarus. He loved to sit around the dinner table with them and talk.

His friend Lazarus became sick and died. So Jesus traveled to Bethany, where Lazarus had been put in a tomb. This was dangerous for Jesus, because people there had once tried to kill him. But Jesus loved his friends too much to let that stop him. When he arrived, he found his friends weeping and mourning Lazarus' death. Jesus was moved to tears himself. Then he demonstrated his power and love by raising Lazarus from the dead.

The good news for us is that Jesus performed this incredible miracle not only for Lazarus and his close friends, but also to teach his followers a very important truth. Jesus used this opportunity to say to us that "everyone who lives and believes in me will never die." This amazing story will show the kids in your class that Jesus gives new life to everyone who believes in him.

a look at the lesson

1. **LISTS OF LOVE** (*10 minutes*)
   Classmates will list ways they're loved by special people in their lives, including Jesus.

2. **NEW LIFE FOR LAZARUS** (*10 minutes*)
   Students will help tell the story of Lazarus being raised from the dead.

3. **I BELIEVE** (*10 minutes*)
   Kids will play a game that emphasizes how important it is to say, "I believe in Jesus."

4. **ALL WRAPPED UP** (*10 minutes*)
   Students will get "all wrapped up" in this game that reviews the story of Lazarus.

5. **THE LAZARUS LEAPER** (*15 minutes*)
   Kids will make a Lazarus figure that "leaps from the tomb."

6. **THE FRAGRANCE OF LIFE** (*5 minutes*)
   Children will pass a bottle of perfume as they take turns praying.

preparation

Gather Bibles, paper, pencils, a chalkboard or newsprint, something fragrant such as perfume, a flashlight, index cards, a timer, markers, a blanket, masking tape, a roll of cloth bandages or string, paper cups, one-by-eleven-inch cardboard strips, wooden clothespins, cotton, and glue.

LISTS OF LOVE

You'll need paper, pencils, a chalkboard or newsprint.

Begin by telling a few personal examples of how special people in your life have shown their love for you. Try to think of examples from when you were the same age as your students.

Form pairs. Say: **Tell your partner about someone who loves you and how that person has shown love for you.**

As kids are sharing, give each student a pencil and a sheet of paper.

Say: **Now write the name of a person who loves you on the top of your paper. Then write down as many ways as you can think of that this person has shown love to you. You might write that the person hugs you when you're sad or takes care of you when you're sick. You'll have about three minutes. Ready? Go!**

After three minutes, have pairs total all the loving acts they listed on their papers. Say: **Wow! It sure looks as though you're loved very much! But if we took all these ways we've listed that we're loved and added them up, they wouldn't even come close to the way Jesus loves us every day.**

Ask:

● What are some ways that Jesus shows his love for us?

Say: Jesus gives us new life and loves us all the time, just as he loved his friends when he was on earth. Let's find out about some of his friends right now.

2. NEW LIFE FOR LAZARUS

Say: We're going to participate in a Bible story about how much Jesus loved his friends. This story comes from the Gospel of John, chapter 11.

> *You'll need a Bible.*

Open your Bible to John 11, and show kids the chapter.

Say: Listen carefully to the story so you can do the actions I tell you to do. This is the story of a man named Lazarus, who got sick and died. His sisters, Mary and Martha, were very sad when he died. Whenever you hear the names "Mary" and "Martha," cover your face, and pretend to sob. When you hear the name "Lazarus," hold your nose, and say, "Pee-yew!" because Lazarus had been dead for days before Jesus arrived. When you hear the word "tomb," lie on the floor with your eyes closed and your hands folded over your chest.

Using an easy-to-understand Bible, read aloud John 11:1-44. Pause to let kids respond to the suggested cues. You may want to use a pencil to underline the key words in your Bible ahead of time. For younger kids you may want to skip verses that are not key to the story or simply paraphrase the entire story.

After you read the story, gather kids in a circle and ask:

● In what ways did Jesus show his love for his friends?
● How does Jesus show his love for you?
● What did Jesus say we need to do to have life?

Say: That's right. Jesus said, "Those who believe in me will have life . . . And everyone who lives and believes in me will never die."

Martha believed that Jesus was the Son of God and had power over death. Jesus brought Lazarus back from the dead to show the glory of God and so that others would believe in him. Let's give Jesus a big cheer for showing us God's glory!

Lead kids in a group cheer for God. Then say: Now let's play a game about believing.

3. I BELIEVE

Say: We learned from the story of Lazarus that if we believe that Jesus is the Son of God, he'll give us new life. We need to believe this before our time is up on earth. Let's play a game to remind us of how

> *You'll need a pencil and eight pieces of scrap paper for each pair of students.*

important it is to believe in Jesus.

Form pairs. Give each pair a pencil and eight pieces of scrap paper. Have pairs print I-B-E-L-I-E-V-E, writing one large letter on each piece of scrap paper. Then collect the papers from each pair.

Mix all of the scraps of paper together, and scatter them in the center of the floor. Say: **On "go," you'll have thirty seconds to work with your partner to find enough letters to spell "I believe." Arrange your papers so that I can read the words. I'll turn off the lights when time is up. Ready? Go!**

Play several rounds as time permits. Then ask:

● **Why were you in such a hurry?**

● **How did you feel when the lights went out before you had gathered all your cards?**

● **How much time do you think you'll have on earth to decide whether you believe in Jesus?**

● **How will you feel if your lights go out before you believe in Jesus?**

● **What do you need to believe in order to have new life?**

Say: **Look at the papers that spell "I believe." Take away the first two letters of "Believe," B and E. Now you have the words "I live" with an E in the middle. That E stands for "Eternal." Eternal means forever, even after your body dies. This is a good way to remember that if you believe in Jesus, you'll live eternally. Now let's find out more about how Jesus gives us new life.**

ALL WRAPPED UP 4.

Say: We're going to have a race I think you can really get "wrapped up" in. This will be a relay race to review the story of Lazarus.

Choose one person in your group to be "Lazarus" first. On "go," wrap the bandage around this person, making sure there are no loose ends to trip the person. Lazarus will hop across the room to the finish line—or tomb. When your team's Lazarus crosses the finish line, count loudly from one to four to symbolize the four days Lazarus was in the tomb. When you finish counting, your Lazarus will hop back to the starting line. Quickly unwrap him or her, and start again with the next person in line. When everyone in your group has had a turn being Lazarus, sit down and yell, "I believe!"

You'll need a roll of cloth bandages or string for each group of four or five students in your class. Before this activity, use masking tape to mark start and finish lines at opposite ends of your room. Form groups of four or five, and have each group sit behind the starting line. Set a roll of bandages in front of each group.

After the race, collect the bandages and ask:

● **Why do you think Jesus waited until Lazarus was in the tomb four days before arriving in Bethany?**

● **Why do you think Jesus chose to raise Lazarus from the dead?**

● **How does it make you feel to know that Jesus has power over death? Explain.**

● **What do you think "believing in Jesus" means?**

Say: Believing in Jesus means accepting that Jesus is the Son of God and that God sent Jesus to earth to give us forgiveness for our sins. He wants us to believe in him and receive his gift of forgiveness. If we do, Jesus will give us new life.

5. THE LAZARUS LEAPER

Say: Jesus said, "Lazarus, come out!" And Lazarus came out of the tomb after being dead four days. This craft will remind us how Lazarus was given new life.

> *For each child, you'll need a paper cup, a one-by-eleven-inch cardboard strip, a wooden clothespin, cotton, a small cloth strip, glue, markers, and a paper wad to cover the top of the cup.*

Help kids follow these instructions for making a Lazarus Leaper. You may want to make one before class so you can show kids what the finished product looks like.

1. Fold the cardboard strip back and forth about eight times, like a spring. Put this into the cup.

2. Glue the cotton on the wooden clothespin figure's head to make a beard and hair. Wrap and glue the cloth around the Lazarus figure like grave clothes. Draw a face on the clothespin with markers.

3. Carefully set the Lazarus figure on the "spring" and compress it so that Lazarus is in the cup.

4. Set the paper wad on top of the opening to represent a stone covering the tomb entrance. When you remove the stone from the tomb, Lazarus will leap from the grave.

When everyone has finished making a Lazarus Leaper, say: **Jesus has power over death. He brought Lazarus back to life after four days in the tomb. Jesus can give you new life, too.**

6. THE FRAGRANCE OF LIFE

Read aloud 2 Corinthians 2:14,16.

> *You'll need a bottle of perfume and a Bible.*

Say: **I'm going to pass around this perfume to remind us of the sweet smell of new life from Jesus.** When you receive the bottle, smell the perfume, and say a simple prayer such as: "Thank you, Jesus, for your gift of new life."

When everyone has prayed, close with your own prayer, asking God to help each student in your class believe in Jesus and receive new life.

Jesus Feeds the Five Thousand

Scripture:
John 6:1-13

Good News:
Jesus wants us to share.

As Jesus' days on earth progressed, he attracted larger and larger crowds. These crowds weren't rich. These crowds weren't relaxing in a comfortable, climate-controlled convention center with peanut vendors in the aisles and concession stands at every turn. These crowds were hungry. They were hungry for spiritual food. And they were hungry for food in their stomachs.

The disciples didn't want to deal with feeding all these people who had come to be near Jesus. Five thousand men were following Jesus. Who knows how many women and children were along with them?

Fortunately, a small boy was willing to share the scant amount of food he had—five loaves of barley bread and two little fish. No amount of sharing was too little for Jesus to bless. No crowd was too big for Jesus to feed.

Jesus had the power to stretch the boy's gift to meet the needs of everyone present that day. He has that same power today. He wants us to share so he can work through our lives and through the lives of those we touch.

a look at the lesson

1. **SHARE SACKS** *(10 minutes)*
   Kids will play a game to try to give away all they have.

2. **POPPIN' PRAISE** *(15 minutes)*
   Kids will enjoy a treat as they hear about the feeding of the five thousand from John 6:1-13.

3. **GIVE-A-HAND RUBBER BANDS** *(10 minutes)*
   Kids will investigate the talents and abilities they can share.

4. **SHARE PRAYERS** *(10 minutes)*
   Students will see how Jesus can "stretch" the things we share.

5. **SHAREPLANE** *(10 minutes)*
   Students will make paper airplanes that use a special sharing power source.

6. **BUBBLE PRAYERS** *(5 minutes)*
   Kids will commit to sharing in the coming week.

preparation

Gather a Bible, microwave popcorn, a bowl, a microwave oven, paper lunch sacks, wide rubber bands, a bag or box, pens or fine-point markers, pencils, yarn, small paper slips, scissors, masking tape, staplers, and bubble solution and bubble wand. You'll also need to make double-sided photocopies of the "Shareplane" handouts (pp. 55-56) on card stock paper. When you make the two-sided handout, be sure the top of each side is at the same end.

SHARE SACKS

You'll need paper lunch sacks, paper slips, yarn, pencils, and scissors.

Give each child a pencil, a paper lunch sack, three paper slips, and a length of yarn long enough to go around the child's waist twice. Have kids write one thing they can share on each paper slip. Then have kids each crumple the slips and put them into their paper lunch sack.

Help each child cut two vertical slits on one side of the sack about three inches from the top of the sack. Weave a piece of yarn through the holes. Tie the child's sack around his or her waist, making sure the sack is behind the child's back.

Say: **On "go," take a paper slip from your sack, and try to "give it away" to another person by putting it into that person's sack. The object is to empty your sack of all slips and sit down. If anyone puts a slip in your sack, you have to get rid of it, too. You have to give** away the slips one at a time, and you need to be careful not to rip any of the paper sacks. If you tear another player's sack, you're out of the game. Are you ready to share? Go!

Call time after a few minutes. Gather kids in a circle and ask:

● **What was it like to give away your paper slips?**

● **Were you able to give away all of the slips in your sack? Why or why not?**

● **In this game, the more slips you gave away, the more slips you received. How is that like what happens when you share in real life?**

Say: **Today, we're going to hear about a hungry crowd and an amazing thing that happened when a little boy decided to share his lunch. Speaking of food, are any of you hungry?**

② POPPIN' PRAISE

Say: Today we're learning that Jesus wants us to share. I have a snack to share with you, but I'm not sure I brought enough. It doesn't look as though this little package of popcorn will make enough for everyone.

Hold up the popcorn package, and ask:

● **Do you think this one little package will make enough for all of us?**

Most kids will be familiar enough with this everyday snack to answer yes. Use their response as part of the object lesson. Ask:

> You'll need microwave popcorn, a bowl, and access to a microwave oven. Before class, bring in enough packages of microwave popcorn to feed your class.

● **How do you know this one package will make enough?** (I've made popcorn before, the bag will get bigger as the popcorn pops, the microwave will make it grow.)

Say: **Well, I'll trust what you say. Let's see what happens.**

Lead your class to the microwave and follow the package directions for cooking the popcorn. Empty the cooked popcorn into a large bowl and say: **Wow! You were right! That little bag of popcorn grew and grew and made enough for all of us. Now let's enjoy it as we hear our Bible story.**

Take kids back to your room, and have them sit in a circle. Pass the bowl of popcorn around the circle as you read aloud John 6:1-13. After you've read the passage, ask:

● **Why didn't Philip think they could feed the large crowd?**

● **What was the disciples' reaction when the boy offered his food?**

Say: **The disciples knew that five loaves and two fish weren't enough to feed a large crowd. But they forgot one very important thing: their power source!**

Ask:

● **Could we have eaten our popped popcorn without putting it in the microwave? Explain.**

● **Could the disciples have fed the crowd without Jesus? Why or why not?**

Say: Just as we needed a power source to pop our popcorn, the disciples needed a power source to turn the boy's food into enough for everyone. Jesus is the power source for our lives. He wants us to share what we have so he can turn it into something bigger. Let's look at some things we can share.

GIVE-A-HAND RUBBER BANDS 3.

Say: The boy in our story had food to share.
Ask:
● What kinds of things can you share?
Say: When we think of things we can share, we usually think of possessions. But we can also share our attitudes and abilities.
Ask:
● What attitudes could you share?
● What happens when you share a positive attitude? when you share a negative attitude?
● What abilities do people share?
● What would the world be like if doctors, and teachers, and ministers kept their abilities to themselves?
Give each student a wide rubber band and a pen or fine-tip marker. Caution kids not to shoot the rubber bands until instructed to do so, and never to shoot them at someone else.
Say: I've given each of you a Give-a-Hand Rubber Band. Write on your rubber band any possessions, attitudes, and abilities that you can share. Write as many as will fit. Nothing is too small or insignificant. Then hold on to your Give-a-Hand Rubber Band when you're finished because we'll use them in the next activity.
When kids finish writing, ask:
● What problems did you have thinking of things to share?
● How do you think the things you wrote could help others?
Say: Jesus gives us all possessions, attitudes, and abilities, and he wants us to share those things. We may not think we have much to offer, but remember the little boy with the loaves and fish? If we plug into the power source as he did, Jesus can make a little go a long way. I'll show you what I mean.

SHARE PRAYERS 4.

Before this activity, use masking tape to mark a starting line on the floor at one end of your room. Set up a box (to use as a target) about five to ten feet away from the line. Have kids hold their rubber bands and line up behind the starting line.

Say: **Jesus wants us to share because he can make what we share go a long way. We're going to take turns shooting our rubber bands at the target. When it's your turn, say this prayer as you shoot your rubberband: "Jesus, help my sharing go a long way!" When everyone has had a turn, we'll collect the rubber bands.**

After each student has had a turn, have kids retrieve their rubber bands. Say: **Just as Jesus stretched the gifts that the boy gave in our story, Jesus will stretch the gifts that you share with others. Turn to a partner, and tell that person one thing you wrote on your rubber band and how sharing that thing could change someone's life.**

Then have kids stand in a close circle with their rubber bands in their right hands. Have them hold onto their neighbor's rubber bands with their left hands.

Say: **Jesus wants us to share. Look at how small our circle is right now. But when we share what we have, our circle grows. Let's take a small step back and watch how our rubber bands stretch. That's how Jesus can stretch what we share.**

Have kids continue stepping back until the rubber bands are stretched as far as is safe and reasonable. Caution kids not to stretch the bands to the breaking point. Say: **Jesus will stretch the gifts we're willing to share. Now let's use these rubber bands to "stretch" our creative talents.**

Have kids put their rubber bands around one of their wrists as they move on to the next activity.

⑤ SHAREPLANE

Say: Let's make paper airplanes. This kind of paper airplane is a little different from most because you can fly it in two different ways. It's a "shareplane."

Use the following instructions to help kids fold, staple, and cut their shareplanes.

1. Hold the shareplane with the art facing up, and fold in half on line A.
2. Open fold, and fold in on lines B and C.
3. Fold line D over flaps.
4. Fold down on line E.
5. Fold in flaps 1 and 2.
6. Fold in line A.
7. Staple where indicated.
8. Cut out slot.
9. Fold back lines F and G.

> *You'll need one "Share-plane" handout (p. 55-56) photocopied onto card stock for each child, scissors, staplers, and the Give-a-Hand Rubber Bands.*

When everyone has finished, take kids to a large, open space such as a fellowship hall or outdoor area. Have kids stand side by side. On "go," have kids launch all their shareplanes at the same time. To avoid injury, make sure kids know to wait for your signal before launching their shareplanes.

After one or two flights, have kids collect their planes and sit. Ask:

● **When you throw a paper airplane, what's the source of power?**

Say: **Your shareplanes went pretty far under your power. But let's try using a stronger power source. Our new power source will be the Give-a-Hand Rubber Bands. Carefully put your rubber band in the special slot we cut out in the plane, and stretch the rubber band away from you. Make sure your shareplane is pointed away from the group, and only launch your plane when I give the signal. Are you ready for countdown?**

Let the kids launch a number of flights. Then gather kids together and ask:

● **How well did your shareplane fly with rubber band power?**

● **How did your rubber band help your shareplanes fly farther?**

● **How does God make your sharing go farther?**

Say: **Jesus wants us to share. When we share, he can use his power to make our sharing go farther. But we need to be willing to share. Let's ask God to help us do that.**

Let kids take their shareplanes home to remind them that Jesus wants us to share.

BUBBLE PRAYERS 6.

You'll need a bottle of bubble solution and a bubble wand.

Have kids sit in a circle. Dip the wand in the bubble solution, and hold it up for kids to see. Ask:

● **This doesn't look like much right now, but what will happen when I blow on the wand?**

Blow a few bubbles, then say: **A bubble isn't expensive or strong, but it usually brings a smile to those who see it. Jesus wants us to share, and when we do he can make beautiful things happen.**

Think of one possession, attitude, or ability you can share this week. We'll pass the bubbles around the circle. When it's your turn, fill in this simple prayer: "Jesus, please help me share my (name a possession, attitude, or ability). Then blow a bubble.

When everyone has blown a bubble, close your time by thanking God for sharing his love with everyone in your class.

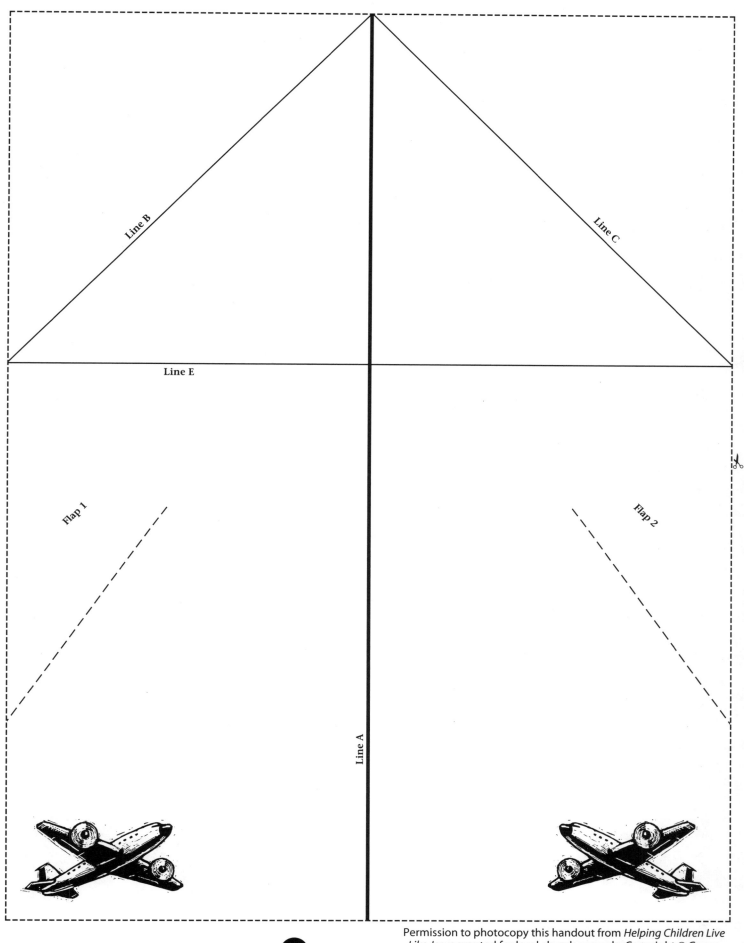

Line B

Line C

Line E

Flap 1

Flap 2

Line A

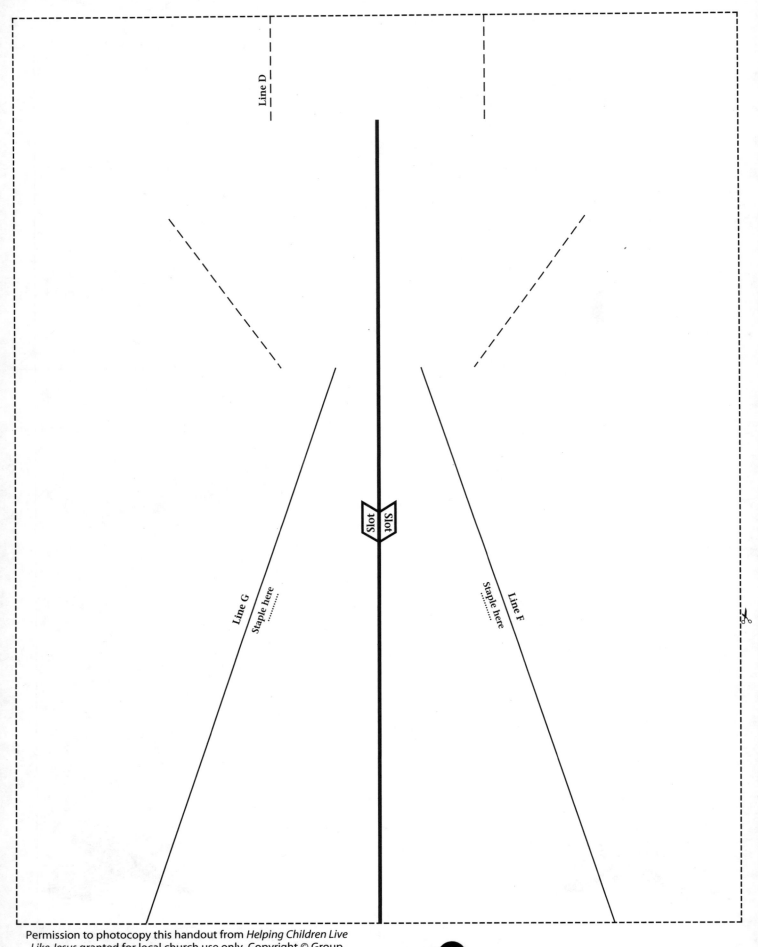

Line D

Line G

Staple here

Slot Slot

Staple here

Line F

Jesus Teaches About Love

Scripture:
Luke 6:27-36

Good News:
We can love others as Jesus loves us.

It's not fair! What a familiar refrain among kids. "It's not fair that Tiffany gets to stay up later"; "it's not fair that Ryan has a nicer bike"; "it's not fair that I got punished, when Cody was the one talking." And if the truth were voiced, you'd probably hear adults making similar statements, such as "It's not fair that Bill got the promotion I deserved."

When we feel wronged, our natural inclination might be to seek revenge—to get even. But Jesus expects more of us. In his Sermon on the Mount, Jesus outlines the way he wants us to live, especially in relation to those who wrong us.

Jesus teaches that it's really not enough to do good to those who are good to you. His standard is higher. Instead of exacting revenge on all the people who hurt him, he died for those very people. He wants us to follow his example. It's tough sometimes, but we can love others as Jesus loves us.

a look at the lesson

1. **KEEP AWAY** (*5 minutes*)
   Kids will play a game to see how it feels to be left out.

2. **CANDY FOR CREEPS?** (*10 minutes*)
   Kids will receive a treat whether they're friendly or not.

3. **"ROLE" WITH THE PUNCHES** (*10 minutes*)
   Students will hear the Bible story from Luke 6 and role play situations.

4. **TUG OR HUG?** (*10 minutes*)
   Kids will enjoy a familiar game with an unexpected twist.

5. **BALANCING BOXERS** (*15 minutes*)
   Kids will make reminders to help them turn the other cheek.

6. **HAPPY HEARTS** (*10 minutes*)
   Students will practice sharing love with everyone.

preparation

Gather Bibles, paper, a bag of wrapped candies, a pencil, snacks, "Balancing Boxer" handouts (p. 62) photocopied onto card stock paper, pennies, scissors, staplers, and heart-shaped candies, erasers, or stickers.

KEEP AWAY 1.

You'll need a paper wad for every three kids in your class.

Form groups of three. Ask:
● How many of you have ever played the game called Keep Away?

Say: Let's play that game right now. Choose who in your threesome will play the person in the middle first. I'll give each group a paper wad. Your job is to toss it back and forth without letting the person in the middle get it. Ready? Go ahead.

After a minute, have kids switch roles and play again. Have them switch roles a third time so everyone gets a chance to be in the middle. Then have kids sit in a circle. Ask:
● How did you feel when you were in the middle during this game?
● When are times in real life you feel left out?
● What do you do when someone hurts your feelings?

Say: This was just a game, but hurt feelings come up often in real life. Today we're learning that we can love others as Jesus loves us. That can be hard to do when we're feeling mad or upset.

2. CANDY FOR CREEPS?

Before class, write each of the following situations on a separate paper slip.

> *You'll need a bag of wrapped candies, paper slips, and a pencil.*

- Act like you're peeling a banana and throwing the peel in front of me.
  - Shake my hand, and say, "You're doing a great job!"
  - Pretend to throw a paper wad at me.
  - Pretend to count out money, and say, "Is this enough?"
  - Shake your finger at me, and pretend to scold me.
  - Pat me on the back, and say, "You tried your best."
  - Pretend you're whispering to a friend and laughing at me.

Say: **To love others as Jesus loves us, first we need to know how Jesus wants us to respond to other people. I need your help for this activity.**

Choose a child to come forward, pick a slip, and act out what's written on it. Choose a new child for each paper slip. If you have less than seven kids in your class, make sure everyone has a turn before letting anyone choose a second slip.

Respond in a friendly way to each student by saying, "Thanks, you're the greatest!" and giving each one a wrapped candy.

When all the slips have been chosen, say: **You've done such a good job of listening, you can all have a treat.**

Give a piece of candy to anyone who didn't receive one earlier. Then ask:

- **What did you think when I gave everyone who came forward a piece of candy?**
- **How would you have responded to these situations in real life?**

Say: **Jesus knew we'd run into all kinds of people, some nice and some not so nice. So he tells us in the Bible how to treat others.**

3. "ROLE" WITH THE PUNCHES

Form groups of four, and give each group a Bible. Say: **Turn in your Bibles to Luke 6:27-36. Choose a Reader in your group and have the Reader read the passage aloud. Listen carefully because we're going to use what we hear.**

> *You'll need Bibles, paper slips, and a pencil.*

When kids have finished reading, say: **Let's play a game of Would You? Should You? Here's how it goes. I'll read a situation, then you'll discuss in your groups what you *would* do in that situation, and what you *should* do. Refer to the Bible passage to back up what you *should* do. We'll share ideas after each situation.**

After reading each situation below, pause to let groups discuss their ideas and then tell their ideas to the rest of the class. Make sure groups use the Bible passage as reference for what they should do in each situation.

- **A bully knocks you down on the playground. What would you do? What should you do?**
- **Your best friend is sitting with someone else at lunch, and won't**

talk to you anymore. What would you do? What should you do?

● You're invited to a friend's birthday party, and have to shop for a present. But you remember that your friend didn't give you a present for your birthday. What would you do? What should you do?

After groups discuss the final situation, say: **We can love others as Jesus loves us. Jesus didn't try to get revenge. He didn't strike back at those who hurt him. He wants us to follow his example.**

TUG OR HUG?

You'll need a snack for each student.

Form two groups.

Say: **Let's play Tug of War—without the rope! We'll play three rounds of twenty seconds each. You'll win the round if you can cause your opponent to lose his or her balance. But be careful not to push or pull too hard. Just use your balance to try to win.**

Huddle with Group 1, and tell them to form a side-by-side line and drop to their knees. Then huddle with Group 2, and tell them that just after the third round of play begins, they should stop tugging and say, "Hey, let's stop tugging and share a snack instead."

When everyone in Group 2 understands the instructions, have them find an opponent from Group 1. Tell opponents to kneel facing each other about an arm's length apart. Have them stretch their arms out in crisscross fashion and hold each other's hands.

Say: **When I flip the lights, tug at your opponent, and try to pull him or her off balance. Anyone who falls off balance will lose that round. I'll flip the lights to signal the end of each round.**

After the third round, flip the lights and distribute the snacks to members of Group 2. Have them share their snacks with their opponents from Group 1. As kids are enjoying their snack, ask:

● **What did you think when your opponent stopped and asked you to share a snack?**

● **Did your opponent's actions change your attitude toward him or her? Explain.**

● **What would you do if you were in an argument with someone and that person suddenly started being nice to you?**

Say: **Jesus wants us to love our enemies. That's hard to do, but with God's help, we can love others as Jesus loves us. This next craft will be a funny reminder of Jesus' instructions.**

BALANCING BOXERS

You'll need one copy of the "Balancing Boxer" hand-

Say: Jesus tells us to "turn the other cheek" when someone wrongs us. Let's make a craft to remind us to turn the other cheek.

Pass out the card stock copies of "The Balancing Boxer." Have kids fold the paper in half at the dotted line and cut out around the solid lines. Then give two pennies to each student.

out (p. 62) photocopied onto card stock paper for each student, two pennies for each student, scissors, and staplers.

Show kids how to put the pennies into the folds of the paper boxing gloves and secure them in place by stapling around the pennies. You may want to make a Balancing Boxer before class so kids can see the finished product.

When kids have finished making their Boxers, show them how to balance the Boxers on their noses. With practice, they can make the Boxers hit them on one cheek. If they turn their heads, they can make the Boxers hit the other cheek.

Say: **Take these Boxers home to remind you that Jesus wants us to love our enemies and turn the other cheek when they hurt us. With his help, we can love others as Jesus loves us.**

6. HAPPY HEARTS

Choose one child to be the Messenger, and give him or her all of the heart-shaped candies, erasers, or stickers. Have the other kids scatter around the room, close their eyes, and hold out a cupped hand.

You'll need one heart-shaped candy, eraser, or sticker for each student.

Say: **This activity will help us practice giving love away. On "go," the Messenger will begin giving away the hearts. As soon as you receive a heart, you may begin walking slowly, but you must keep your eyes closed. When you bump into someone, open your eyes and give your heart to that person, then close your eyes and stand still. Sometimes you may have more than one heart, but you may only give away one heart at a time.**

Once the Messenger has given away all the hearts, have him or her help guide any child who is heading away from the group or who's about to run into something. After three minutes, have kids open their eyes. Give every child a candy, and have kids sit in a circle. Ask:

● **In this activity, could you choose who you wanted to give your candy heart to? Why or why not?**

● **What was it like to give your candy to just anyone?**

Say: **Jesus says we need to love everyone, not just the people who love us.** Ask:

● **How can we love our enemies?**

Say: **We can use Jesus as our example of how to love everyone, even those people who don't love us. Think of someone you might be having a problem with. Don't say the person's name aloud; just think of that person's name. As we go around the circle, tell one way you can show love to that person this week.**

When everyone in the circle has spoken, close in prayer, thanking God that we can love others as Jesus loves us.

Balancing Boxer

TURN THE
OTHER CHEEK

Jesus' Triumphal Entry Into Jerusalem

Scripture:
Mark 11:1-11

Good News:
We can praise and honor Jesus in our daily lives.

The streets of Jerusalem were full. A parade of people, palm branches, and praises filled the city with excitement. Jesus rode into the city on a colt as the prophet Zechariah had said he would. The disciples followed in awe of the praises offered to their master.

People placed coats on the path and shouted hosannas in praise. The kingdom of God was at hand. Everyone stopped what they were doing to offer praise in honor of Jesus' entry into Jerusalem.

Praise and honor filled the streets that day in Jesus' life. But can praise and honor go beyond the walls of the church today? To some they seem to belong only in a worship service. Children learn praise songs in Sunday school, but it is a fortunate child who is taught to praise and honor Jesus at home. Not every child has this advantage.

In this lesson, students will discover ways to praise and honor Jesus in their daily lives.

a look at the lesson

1. **COLORFUL COATS** *(10 minutes)*
   Students will make cutout coats and will decorate them with words of praise.

2. **ON THE ROAD AGAIN** *(10 minutes)*
   Children will make a road with their cutout coats while they listen to Mark 11:1-11.

3. **COATS ACROSS** *(12 minutes)*
   Kids will use the coats in a race and will discuss how they can honor God.

4. **HEAD, HEART, AND HANDS** *(10 minutes)*
   Kids will list ways to honor God as they hear Colossians 3:23.

5. **HANG-UPS** *(10 minutes)*
   Children will pray as they "hang up" their coats on the wall.

6. **PUT-ONS** *(8 minutes)*
   Kids will put on an old coat and share new ways they'll honor Jesus.

preparation

 Gather Bibles, paper grocery sacks, scissors, markers, scraps of cloth and yarn, glue sticks, pencils, and photocopies of the "Honor Jesus" handout (p. 68). You'll also need yarn or string, strong tape or thumbtacks, clip clothespins, an old coat, a cassette player, and a cassette of children's praise music.

COLORFUL COATS 1.

> *You'll need a large paper grocery sack for each child, scraps of cloth and yarn, glue sticks, scissors, and markers.*

Give each child a grocery sack. Provide scissors, markers, glue sticks, and scraps of cloth and yarn. Say: **Today we're going to learn about a special day when Jesus went to Jerusalem. The people who greeted him used their coats to make a path for him as he entered the city. Let's make coats to use for this Bible story.**

Show children how to cut out armholes and a neck hole from the sides and bottom of the sack. Then have them make a center vertical cut down the front from the neck hole to the open bottom of the sack. Use the illustration in the margin as a guide.

Once kids cut out the coat shapes, have kids decorate them with markers and the scraps of cloth and yarn. Encourage kids to write praise phrases such as "God is awesome!" or "Jesus is great!" on their coats. Say: **The people in Jerusalem were excited to see Jesus. They had heard a lot about him. Let's make our coats bright and colorful to show how happy the people were the day Jesus entered Jerusalem.**

Give children a few minutes to complete their coats. When everyone is ready, have children sit in a circle. Give each child an opportunity to show his or her coat. Have children admire each other's art work. Ask:

● **What do you do with a real coat?**
● **Why would someone put a coat on the ground?**

Say: **We're going to find out why people wanted to put their coats on the ground in our story today. We'll also discover that we can praise and honor Jesus in our daily lives.**

2. ON THE ROAD AGAIN

Have children place their Colorful Coats on the floor in a long winding path around the room. Say: **We're going to travel along this road while we listen to the Bible story. You'll need to listen carefully as I read the verses. Every time I say a movement word, take one step forward. Let's practice. I'll read the first verse.**

> You'll need a Bible and the Colorful Coats from the previous activity.

Read Mark 11:1 and pause after the word "coming." Then say: **Good. You're ready to move. Listen as I read from Mark, chapter 11, verses 1 through 11.**

Read aloud the verses, pausing at the italicized words to allow kids to take a step forward on the path.

Say: "As Jesus and his followers were *coming* closer to Jerusalem, they *came* to the towns of Bethphage and Bethany near the Mount of Olives. From there Jesus *sent* two of his followers and said to them, '*Go* to the town you can see there. When you *enter* it, you will quickly find a colt tied, which no one has ever ridden. Untie it and *bring* it here to me. If anyone asks you why you are doing this, tell him its Master needs the colt. He will *send* it at once.'

"The followers *went* into the town, found a colt tied in the street near the door of a house, and untied it. Some people were standing there and asked, 'What are you doing? Why are you untying that colt?' The followers answered the way Jesus told them to answer, and the people let them *take* the colt.

"They *brought* the colt to Jesus and put their coats on it, and Jesus sat on it. Many people spread their coats on the road. Others cut branches in the fields and spread them on the road. The people were *walking* ahead of Jesus. [Others were *following*] him, shouting, 'Praise God! God bless the one who comes in the name of the Lord! God bless the kingdom of our father David! That kingdom is *coming!*'

"Jesus *entered* Jerusalem and *went* into the Temple. After he had looked at everything, since it was already late, he *went* out to Bethany with the twelve apostles."

Have children find their own coats and sit on them in a large circle. Ask:

● **What was it like to travel around the path during our story?**
● **How do you think the people who were walking with Jesus felt?**

Say: **The people who met Jesus showed him honor by praising him with words and actions. They shouted "hosanna" and put their** coats at his feet. When we honor someone, we show them that they are special to us. Ask:

- **What does it mean to honor Jesus?**
- **How do you honor Jesus?**

Say: **Let's play a game that will help us honor Jesus.**

COATS ACROSS ③.

You'll need a Bible and the Colorful Coats.

Have a volunteer read aloud Luke 19:32-36. Ask:
- **Who is mentioned in this verse?**

Say: **That's right: Jesus, his followers, a crowd, and a colt. We're going to have a race to get to Jerusalem.**

Form groups of four. Have each group choose two Colorful Coats to use. Then have groups line up at one end of the room. Say: **Each group will need to choose one person to be a "colt" and one person to be "Jesus." You don't have to sit on the colt's back; you'll just stay together. The other two in each group are the "front and back movers." You'll be moving the coats. Each time you move a coat, someone in your group will say a way to honor God.**

Show groups how to begin by using one group to demonstrate. Have the two children chosen to be Jesus and the colt stand on the front coat. Have the back mover hold the other coat until someone in the group mentions a way to honor God. Then have the back mover pass the coat to the front mover. The front mover will place the coat on the floor so the colt and Jesus can step forward onto it. Continue playing until all groups have reached "Jerusalem," or the other side of the room. Then ask:

- **Was this game easy or difficult? Explain.**
- **Is it easy or difficult to honor Jesus?**
- **How can we honor Jesus in our daily lives?**

Say: **Let's find out more about honoring God.**

HEAD, HEART, AND HANDS ④.

You'll need Bibles, one copy of the "Honor Jesus" handout (p. 68) for each child, and pencils.

Have children stay in their groups of four. Give each group a Bible, four pencils, and four copies of the "Honor Jesus" handout. Have each group choose one member to be the "head," one to be the "hands," another to be the "heart," and one to be the "feet."

Say: **In your group, brainstorm about ways we can honor Jesus with our heads, hearts, hands, and feet. A verse is written beside each part. Read the verses, then help each other think of and write one idea for each part.**

Give groups five minutes to work on their handouts. Then bring everyone together, and have groups take turns telling ideas.

Say: **You've thought of wonderful ways to honor Jesus!**
Have a child read aloud Colossians 3:23. Then ask:
● **According to this verse, when can we honor Jesus?**

Say: **In everything, no matter what we're doing, we can praise and honor Jesus in our daily lives. Wow! That makes it exciting to think that jumping rope, helping Mom make dinner, or washing your dog can show Jesus honor. It's all in your attitude as you go through your day and dedicate each activity to him. Let's spend time dedicating our Colorful Coats to him.**

⑤ HANG-UPS

Have kids stand and hold their Colorful Coats.
Say: **We've made these special coats as reminders of how we can praise and honor Jesus in our lives. Let's hang them up so everyone can see them.**

You'll need the Colorful Coats, yarn or string, strong tape or thumb-tacks, and clip clothespins.

Have kids help you tape or tack a strand of yarn or string around the room, four to five feet above the floor. Place the yarn "clothesline" lower for smaller children. Help children hang their coats on the clothesline.

Then pray: **God, we want to praise and honor you every day. Help us use these coats as reminders of things we can do at home, at school, and at church. In Jesus' name. Amen.**

Leave the coats up for a few weeks. Later, encourage kids to take them home to hang in their rooms as reminders that they can praise and honor Jesus in their daily lives.

⑥ PUT-ONS

Have the children stand in a circle. Hold up the old coat, and say: **We're going to take turns putting on this old coat while we play a game. The game is called Musical Coats, and we play it almost like Musical Chairs. We'll pass the coat around and each person will put it on while the music plays. If you're wearing the coat when the music stops, you're not out. Instead, you get a chance to tell one way you'll honor Jesus this week. Let's play!**

You'll need an old coat, a cassette player, and a cassette of children's praise music.

Begin the music, and start the game by putting the coat on, taking it off, and passing it to the child on your right. Time the music to stop so every child gets a chance to speak. Play until everyone has worn the coat and told an idea.

Say: **We can praise and honor Jesus every day this week. Let's join hands and yell "Yeah, God!" as a group cheer.**

Honor Jesus

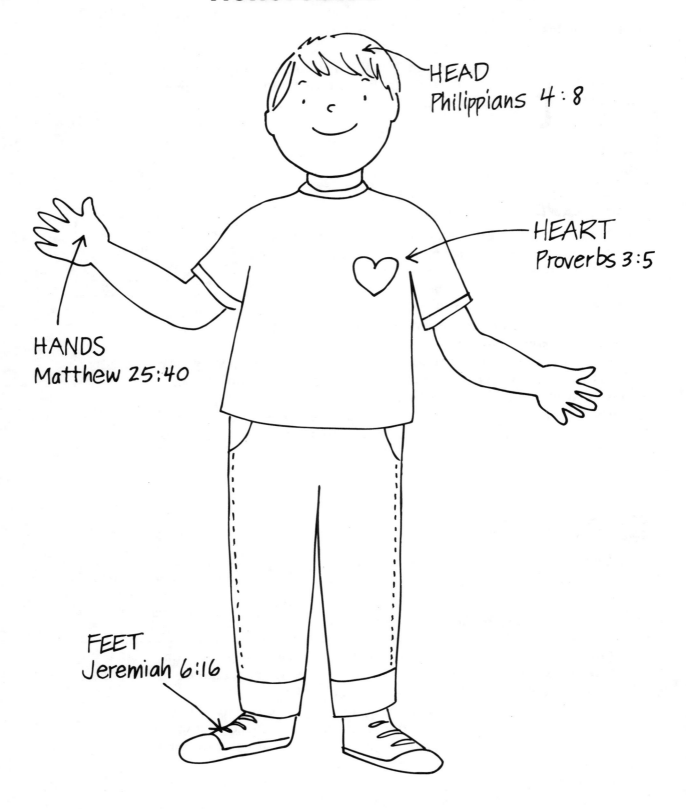

HEAD
Philippians 4:8

HEART
Proverbs 3:5

HANDS
Matthew 25:40

FEET
Jeremiah 6:16

The Last Supper

Scripture:
Matthew 26:26-35;
John 13:1-20

Good News:
We can serve Jesus
by serving others.

As Jesus shared his last meal on earth with his disciples, he suddenly got up from the table. He wrapped a towel around his waist and washed his friends' feet. Some of them allowed him to, but Peter resisted. Jesus explained that if he, as Lord and teacher, washed his disciples' feet, they should also wash each other's feet. Jesus wanted to give his followers a picture of servanthood—a way to express love to God. Jesus gave a simple pattern to follow: Serve others.

Service can seem tedious—setting the table, making a bed, taking out the garbage, for example. Service isn't glamorous at all. Helping older people eat a meal, reading to young children, and dishing out soup at a shelter for the homeless don't seem like big things to do for God. But they are!

This lesson will help kids realize that as we serve others, we are also serving God.

a look at the lesson

1. **THROW IN THE TOWELS** *(10 minutes)*
    Children will tear up a towel to create personal service towels.

2. **TOWEL TIME** *(10 minutes)*
    Children will listen to the story of the Last Supper from John 13:1-20 in a fun way.

3. **FEET AND MORE** *(10 minutes)*
    Kids will think of ways to serve others in difficult situations.

4. **THREE STRIKES—YOU'RE NOT OUT!** *(10 minutes)*
    Kids will listen to Matthew 26:26-35 and 1 John 1:9 and then create a visual expression of God's forgiveness.

5. **SHOESHINE** *(10 minutes)*
    Kids will pair up for a shoeshine service game and listen to Mark 10:44.

6. **SERVICE NEWS** *(10 minutes)*
    Children will brainstorm about service ideas to use in their neighborhoods.

preparation

Gather a Bible, old bath towels, scissors, permanent markers, newsprint, tape, pencils, and photocopies of the "Feet and More" handout (p. 74).

THROW IN THE TOWELS

> *You'll need old bath towels, scissors, and permanent markers. You'll need one towel for every six children. Before class, make one-inch cuts on the sides of the towels to allow children to rip the towels into six wide pieces.*

Say: Today we'll learn about the last supper Jesus shared with his friends before he died. Jesus did something that surprised his friends. If you know what he did, keep it a secret. If you don't know, you'll find out soon. I'll tell you this: He used a towel. So we're going to make towels to use, too.

Form groups of six, and give each group one of the prepared towels. Have kids take turns ripping off one section of the towels until each child has a small rectangular towel. Have kids use markers to personalize their towels by writing their names or drawing pictures on them. Have kids each draw a cross on the towel as well. Ask:

- What are ways we could use these towels to help others?
- How do you think Jesus used a towel during the Last Supper?

Say: Jesus wanted to be a servant to his friends. Even though he was God, he gave up everything in heaven to come to earth to serve us. He served us by loving us enough to die on the cross. Being a servant means helping others. We can serve Jesus by serving others. Let's see what serving is all about.

2. TOWEL TIME

Say: The story of the Last Supper is found in John 13:1-20. As we read it, use your towels and your feet to tell the story. First, take off your shoes.

Give kids time to take off their shoes and socks.

Say: Every time you hear the word "feet," wiggle your toes. Whenever you hear the word "towel," pass your towel to the person on your right. After the story is over, we'll return the towels to their owners.

Read the following story adapted from John 13:1-20. Pause at the italicized words to allow children to respond to the words "feet" and "towel."

Say: Jesus planned a special way for his friends to celebrate the Passover meal. He loved his friends very much, and he knew it was almost time for him to die. While they were eating supper, Jesus took off his coat and picked up a *towel*. He washed his friends' *feet*. Then Jesus dried their *feet* with the *towel*. When he came to Peter, Peter said, "No! You shouldn't wash my *feet*. I should wash your *feet*." But Jesus explained that he must wash Peter's *feet* so that Peter could be one of his people. When Jesus washed all their *feet*, he put down the *towel* and said, "Do you know why I washed your *feet* with a *towel?* If your Lord washes your *feet*, then you should wash each other's *feet*."

Ask:
- Why do you think people washed feet during Jesus' day?
- Why did Jesus wash his friends' feet?

Say: During biblical times, most people wore sandals and lived where the ground was covered with sand. So feet got hot and dirty. When someone came to a house to visit, a slave or servant would wash and dry the tired feet of the visitor. Jesus was showing his disciples that he was willing to be their servant.

We don't live in a desert or wear sandals all the time, so washing feet may not be what Jesus would want us to do for others. Let's think of other ways we can serve Jesus by serving others.

Have kids return the towels to their owners. Kids may put their socks back on, but they'll need their shoes off later in the lesson.

> You'll need a Bible and the towels from the "Throw in the Towels" activity.

> **TEACHER TIP**
>
> Some children may not want to remove their shoes and socks. Encourage those children to wiggle their fingers instead of their toes. Also, if you feel your class is mature enough, you could provide dishpans of warm water and have kids actually wash and dry each other's feet.

3. FEET AND MORE

Gather children in a circle, and hand out pencils and the "Feet and More" handouts. Make sure each child has his or her towel from the first activity.

Say: Jesus told his friends to wash each other's feet, but he meant more than that. He wanted his friends to serve others. Let's find ways to serve besides washing feet. We'll read each situation on our papers.

> You'll need pencils, the towels from the "Throw in the Towels" activity, and one photocopy of the "Feet and More" handout (p. 74) for each child.

When you think of a way to serve in that situation, wave your towel in the air. We'll fill in our "Feet and More" handouts together.

Read the first situation, and wait for someone to wave a towel. Allow a few responses for each situation. Encourage kids to write the suggestions on their handouts. When everyone has responded and all situations have been completed, say: **We can serve Jesus by serving others in lots of ways. In our story from the Gospel of John, remember how Peter didn't want Jesus to wash his feet? Peter didn't understand what Jesus meant about serving others, but he was learning. Jesus was patient with Peter because he knew that Peter would be a great servant once he'd learned to serve others. We're going to find out a hard lesson Peter had to learn before Jesus died.**

THREE STRIKES—YOU'RE NOT OUT! 4.

You'll need a Bible, towels from the "Throw in the Towels" activity, and markers.

Say: The lesson Peter learned is found in Matthew 26:26-35.

Read the passage aloud, then ask:

● **What did Jesus say that Peter would do three times before the rooster crowed?**

● **How do you think Peter felt when Jesus said that?**

Set out markers. Say: **Take your towel, and make three slash marks on it with a marker.** Give children time to make the marks, then say: **Peter *did* tell people that he didn't know Jesus. He did it three times before the rooster crowed, just as Jesus said he would. The marks on your towel represent the three times Peter denied Jesus.**

Ask:

● **Have you ever done something to hurt someone?**

● **How did that person treat you afterward?**

● **How did you feel about what you had done?**

● **How do you think Peter felt after he denied Jesus?**

Have a child read aloud 1 John 1:9. Ask:

● **According to this verse, when we do something wrong, what do we need to do?**

● **What does it mean to "confess our sins"?**

● **What will God do if we confess our sins?**

Say: **Now think of three things you've done wrong recently. You don't have to say anything out loud, just think of three things you're sorry for. Silently pray, and ask Jesus to forgive you for those three things.**

Give kids a few moments to pray. Then say: **Because Jesus was willing to be a servant and go to the cross for us, our sins can be forgiven. Take a marker, and turn the slashes on your towels into crosses.**

Wait a few moments, then say: **There's an old song you probably know, but we're going to change the words just a little. The new words will be "For it's one, two, three strikes, you're not out! 'Cause**

Jesus loves you!" We'll sing it to the tune of "Take Me Out to the Ball Game."

Lead children in singing the last two lines of the song with the new words. Encourage kids to yell out the numbers.

5. SHOESHINE

Have kids put all their shoes in a pile in the middle of the room. Form pairs. Have a child read aloud Mark 10:44.

You'll need a Bible, towels from the "Throw in the Towels" activity, and everyone's shoes.

Say: **Even though we all don't need to have our feet washed, we do need our shoes shined. Find your partner's shoes, and polish them lightly with your towel.**

On "go," have one partner from each pair go to the pile to find the other partner's shoes. When they return, have them assist their partners in putting on their shoes. Then have the other partners go find their partners' shoes. Once everyone has shoes on again, have partners shine each other's shoes with their towels.

Say: **We can serve Jesus by serving others. To finish, let's brainstorm about ways we can commit to serving others this week.**

6. SERVICE NEWS

Tape the newsprint to the wall, and have children sit in front of it. Say: **We've learned that we can serve Jesus by serving others. Now we need to decide how we'll do that. Let's see how many ways to serve others**

You'll need a large sheet of newsprint, tape, markers, and scissors.

this week we can think of. When you think of a way to serve, you'll stand and act out the action—without words—and we'll try to guess what you're doing.

Encourage each child to take a turn standing and acting out his or her idea. If the class is unable to guess the action, have the child tell the service idea. It's OK if more than one child acts out the same idea. Write all ideas on the newsprint. Then ask children to pick one way they'll serve others during the coming week. Cut apart the newsprint so each child has a written idea to take home.

Say: **Take your reminder home with you, and this week, try to do what it says to serve others. Take your towel home, too. You may want to use it to serve others, or you can keep it as a reminder. Just remember: We can serve Jesus by serving others.**

Feet and More

Read each situation, and think of a way you could help.

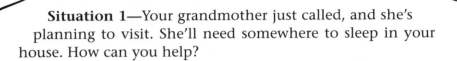

Situation 1—Your grandmother just called, and she's planning to visit. She'll need somewhere to sleep in your house. How can you help?

Situation 2—Two of your friends are mad at each other and won't talk. What can you do?

Situation 3—New people are moving into a house on your block. They look lonely. How could you use your towel to help them?

Situation 4—The church is having a special dinner, and a lot of people will be eating in the fellowship hall. What could you do to help?

Situation 5—There are people in your community who don't have enough food or clothes. How can you help?

"If I, your Lord and Teacher, have washed your feet, you also should wash each other's feet" (John 13:14).

Jesus Dies on the Cross

Scripture:
Matthew
26:36–27:56

Good News:
We have forgiveness through Jesus' death.

On the night of his arrest, Jesus took a few of his disciples to a peaceful garden. As he prayed, they slept. Marching feet and loud voices awoke the disciples. Judas, one of Jesus' own, met the Master with a kiss of betrayal, and the disciples watched helplessly as guards marshaled their Lord away into the night. The nightmare continued as Jesus was taken before Pilate. Peter, who had vowed that he would die with Jesus if need be, denied ever knowing his Savior—not once, but three times. Finally, the guards led Jesus out of the city to die on a cross, crucified between two common criminals.

This sad story is hard to tell to children. We want to sugarcoat what happened, but it's not necessary. Kids need to know that Jesus willingly sacrificed his life for us so our sins can be forgiven. And don't forget to offer a little hint about the following lesson. Jesus died so we can be forgiven, then he rose again so we can have eternal life.

In this lesson, students will understand that we have forgiveness through Jesus.

a look at the lesson

1. **STOLEN AWAY** *(10 minutes)*
   Students will pray and learn how it feels to have their teacher taken away suddenly.

2. **SLEEPING ON THE JOB** *(10 minutes)*
   Children will act out parts of the story of Jesus' death.

3. **CROW AND GO** *(10 minutes)*
   Kids will hear Matthew 27:69-75 and go on a treasure hunt for eggs with a message.

4. **CROSS MY HEART** *(10 minutes)*
   Kids will list sins and thank yous to God on a cutout cross.

5. **IN THE TOMB** *(10 minutes)*
   Children will crawl in a "tomb" and thank Jesus for giving his life.

6. **PASS IT ON** *(10 minutes)*
   Kids will play a whispering game of hope that teaches about the Resurrection.

preparation

Gather a Bible, pillows, blankets, masking tape, twelve plastic eggs or small paper sacks, a permanent marker, paper, photocopies of the "Cross My Heart" handout (p. 81), markers, pens, scissors, pencils, a large box, and a chalkboard or newsprint. You'll also need two adult volunteers for the first activity. If possible, choose someone the children don't know.

STOLEN AWAY

You'll need a Bible and two adult volunteers, one to "take you away" and another to stay with your class. Plan to rejoin the kids after they pray.

Say: We're going to hear what happened to Jesus when he went to pray in a garden one night. This story is recorded in Matthew 26.

Open your Bible to Matthew 26, and show kids the chapter.

Say: **Jesus took his disciples with him to a place called Gethsemane. Jesus had most of the disciples sit and wait for him, but he asked Peter, James, and John to walk with him into the garden a little way. He was sad and wanted them to wait with him while he prayed. Jesus walked a little farther away and began to pray. Peter, James, and John were tired.** *(Have children all yawn and stretch.)* **The three disciples fell asleep.** *(Encourage children to lie down and pretend to sleep.)* **All of a sudden** *(Let this be the cue for the interruption. Encourage the volunteer to be abrupt, almost rude, as he or she demands that you come away.)*

Have the other adult helper continue by asking:

- **What do you think that was all about?**
- **How did it make you feel?**
- **Why do you think** (leader's name) **had to leave?**

Say: **Let's pray and then maybe we'll find out.**

Pray: **Dear God, sometimes things happen that surprise us, and we don't know what to think. Help us listen to the Bible story to find out more about Jesus. Thank you. Amen.**

Rejoin the group, and ask:
- **How did you feel when I had to leave suddenly?**
- **What did you think was going to happen?**

Say: **Jesus' disciples were scared and didn't know what to do when he disappeared suddenly. Let's gather some props to help us tell our Bible story.**

② SLEEPING ON THE JOB

Say: As I read the Bible story, move from corner to corner acting out what the disciples did. I'll help by giving you cues.

Read the following story adapted from Matthew 26:36–27:56. Pause to allow children time for moving from corner to corner and acting out the story.

Say: **After the Last Supper, Jesus went out for a walk with his disciples.** (*Have children walk around in a circle in the middle of the room.*) **He stopped at a beautiful garden called Gethsemane.** (*Have children move toward the corner of the room with blankets and pillows.*) **"Please wait while I pray," Jesus said and walked farther into the garden. While Jesus went to pray, the disciples began to feel tired. They yawned and stretched and soon fell asleep.** (*Encourage children to yawn, stretch, and then curl up with the pillows and blankets.*) **When Jesus came back, he found his friends asleep. So Jesus left them and went to pray again because he was sad and knew that soon he would be taken away and killed. Jesus went to pray three times. Each time he came back to his friends, they were asleep.** (*Have children pretend to be asleep.*)

> You'll need pillows, blankets, and masking tape. A large, empty room will work best for this activity; if you use a classroom, move all the chairs and tables to one side. Before class, make three masking tape crosses on the wall in one corner of the room. Put a chair in a second corner. Have children place all the pillows and blankets in another corner of the room. Leave the last corner empty.

Then suddenly, a group of soldiers came up with one of Jesus' friends, Judas. (*Have the kids act surprised.*) **The soldiers grabbed Jesus. The disciples were angry and upset.** (*Have children jump up and act angry and upset.*) **But Jesus didn't fight back or get mad. He went with the soldiers, and the disciples ran away.** (*Have children run to the middle of the room.*)

Jesus was taken to the leaders of the land. (*Have children walk toward the corner with the chair in it.*) **The disciples were so scared. They were hiding.** (*Have children squat down and cover their heads as if hiding.*) **The rulers and crowds decided to kill Jesus. They took Jesus, along**

with two robbers, to a hill outside the city and put them on three crosses. *(Have children go to the corner with crosses.)* **The disciples cried and kept hiding when they found out what was happening. They were so sad.** *(Encourage children to sit quietly by the crosses.)* **The disciples felt all alone.** *(Have children go to the empty corner and sit quietly.)*

Ask:

● **How do you think the disciples felt when Jesus was taken away from them?**

● **How would you have felt?**

Say: **This is a sad story. But I'll tell you a secret—it has a very happy ending! Because of Jesus' death, we've been given a wonderful gift from God. We'll find out more about that gift by having a treasure hunt.**

CROW AND GO 4.

You'll need a Bible, twelve plastic eggs, a permanent marker, and paper. If you can't find plastic eggs, use small paper sacks instead. Plan to use a separate room for this activity. If weather permits, enjoy this egg hunt outside. Before class, write one word from Colossians 1:14 on each of twelve small paper slips. Put one word in each plastic egg, and use a marker to number the eggs on the outside. Number the eggs in the same sequence as the words from the verse. Hide the eggs around the room.

Say: When Jesus was arrested, all the disciples ran away. But Peter watched from a distance and followed the soldiers to see where they were taking Jesus. Peter hid outside of the building where Jesus was being held prisoner.

Have children take turns reading aloud the verses from Matthew 26:69-75.

Say: **Peter was sad because he told people he didn't know Jesus. Jesus forgave Peter just as he forgives us when we do wrong things. Forgiveness is a treasure from God. Let's have an Easter egg hunt to find a special treasure.**

Form twelve groups. A group can be one person. Tell each group to choose someone to be the Farmer. The rest of the group will be the Roosters. Number the groups. Then say: **Each group will look for a plastic egg with their group's number on it. Roosters, your job will be to walk around looking for eggs. When you see one, you'll start crowing. The Farmer from your group will come and pick up the egg to see if it has the same number as your group. If the number matches, the Farmer will run to the front and bring the egg to me. If it's not the right number, keep on looking!** If you have fewer than twelve kids, just choose one farmer for the entire class.

When all the eggs have been gathered, have children sit in a semicircle as they open their plastic eggs. Then help kids put the words of the verse in proper order, and have a child read the verse aloud. Ask:

● **What did Jesus do for us?**

● **What did he give us when he died for us?**

● **How can we receive his gift?**

Say: We can have forgiveness through Jesus' death. Jesus took all our sins with him to the cross. So he paid for all the bad things we do. We can have forgiveness when we tell Jesus we're sorry. We can receive his gift when we simply accept it. That's why what happened on the cross is so important.

4. CROSS MY HEART

Give each child a copy of the "Cross My Heart" handout. Set out pencils, pens, scissors, and markers. Encourage children to cut out the crosses from the handout.

> *You'll need a Bible, photocopies of the "Cross My Heart" handout (p. 81), scissors, markers, pens, and pencils.*

Say: **We can have forgiveness for all the wrong things we do when we ask Jesus to forgive us.**

Ask:

● **What are some wrong things people do?**

Say: **Turn your crosses over so you can't see the heart shape. Using a pencil, write some of the wrong things you've done or things you know are wrong to do.**

Give kids a few moments to list sins. Then say: **Now turn your crosses over, and use markers to write a thank you note to God for his forgiveness.**

After children complete their crosses, say: **When Jesus died on the cross, he was buried and stayed in the tomb for three days. It was a very sad time for the disciples. They didn't understand why he had to die. But we know that it was to pay the price for our sins. So we're thankful that Jesus was willing to go through all the pain and loneliness of dying on the cross so we can be forgiven. Let's spend a few minutes thanking God.**

5. IN THE TOMB

Place the box in the center of the room. Have children form a circle around the box. Say: **After Jesus died on the cross, his body was placed in a tomb. We're going to pretend this box is a tomb. We'll take turns crawling inside to thank Jesus for giving up his life so we can have forgiveness.**

> *You'll need a Bible and a large cardboard box big enough for a child to crawl inside.*

As children take turns entering the "tomb," encourage them to say a short prayer of thanks while they're inside. Sing a chorus of thanksgiving with the children as they wait for their turns to enter the tomb. Choose a song such as "Alleluia," and continue changing the verses as each child takes a turn. Use verses such as "Jesus loves us" or "God forgives us."

After everyone has had a turn, have a child read aloud 1 Peter 3:18. Ask:

● Why did Jesus have to die?

● What can we do to let Jesus know we're thankful for his forgiveness?

Say: That's right. Praying and telling God thank you for his forgiveness is important. We have forgiveness through Jesus' death, but that's not the end of the story. Let me give you a hint about what happens next.

PASS IT ON 6.

> You'll need a Bible and a chalkboard or newsprint.

Form a circle.

Say: We're going to play a game that has an important message at the end. First we'll practice a few times to make sure we can do this. Someone will start a phrase by whispering to the person on his or her right. Then that person will skip two people and tell the next person. Then the message will skip over three people, then four, then five, until everyone knows. As soon as you've heard the message, stand with your hands above your head. When everyone has their hands up, the last person to receive the message can yell it out loud.

Let kids practice with simple messages such as "Mary had a little frog," or "Simple Simon met the Donut Man." Be prepared for laughs and giggles.

Then begin the real message: "Jesus will rise from the dead." Let kids whisper the message through the group. When the last person has repeated the message, correct it if necessary, and have everyone repeat it together. Write it on the chalkboard or newsprint, then have a child read aloud Matthew 26:31-32. Ask:

● What do you think the disciples thought when Jesus said this?

Say: Jesus spoke to his disciples about his death the night he was arrested. He also told them that he would rise from the dead, but they didn't understand. We'll find out more about Jesus' resurrection in another lesson. Until then, remember that this story has a happy ending!

Cross My Heart

Jesus Is Risen!

Scripture:
Matthew 28:1-10

Good News:
We're happy that
Jesus is alive
today!

Early morning light streaked across the horizon as Mary Magdalene and Mary walked toward the tomb where Jesus' body had lain. When they reached the tomb, they found the stone rolled away from the door, soldiers shaking with fear, and an angel sitting on top of the stone. "Jesus is risen from death," Mary Magdalene and Mary were told. Amazed and yet thrilled at the prospect, the women gladly followed the angel's instructions to hurry and tell Jesus' followers the good news. The women ran off feeling afraid, but very happy.

Children love good news. And this is the best news ever! Sharing the joy of the Resurrection provides a party atmosphere of celebration. Encourage children to rejoice.

This lesson lets children know that we can be happy that Jesus is alive today!

a look at the lesson

1. **FREEZE PHRASE** *(10 minutes)*
   Kids will play a game where the good news about Jesus will set them free.

2. **EARTHQUAKE, ANGEL, STONE** *(10 minutes)*
   Students will enjoy an interactive story from Matthew 28:1-10.

3. **EGGSTRA! EGGSTRA!** *(10 minutes)*
   Children will discover empty eggs as they listen to Mark 16:1-6.

4. **MOSAIC MASTERPIECES** *(10 minutes)*
   Children will make mural mosaics to celebrate the good news that Jesus is alive today.

5. **SONRISE SONG** *(10 minutes)*
   Kids will use words from Matthew 28:1-10 to write a song about the Resurrection.

6. **EGG-SALAD CELEBRATION** *(10 minutes)*
   Kids will make egg-salad sandwiches to celebrate the Resurrection together.

preparation

Gather Bibles, feathers, small rocks, newspapers, bowls, craft glue, poster board, pencils, a cassette recorder, a blank cassette tape, photocopies of the "Sonrise Song" handout (p. 89), bread, plastic knives, mayonnaise, a large mixing bowl, mixing spoons, paper plates, napkins, and a drink. You'll also need one additional colored egg for each child. Prepare the eggs before class by hard-boiling half of them and blowing out the contents of the uncooked eggs. To blow out the uncooked eggs, simply make a needle hole at the top and bottom, and blow whites and yokes into a bowl. You can save whites and yolks to make scrambled eggs! Then color all the eggs, being especially careful with the empty ones. Refrigerate the eggs.

FREEZE PHRASE

> You'll need a small craft feather for each child and one rock. Play this game in a large open area if possible.

Say: We learned that Jesus died on the cross and was buried. Today we'll find out what happened on the third day after that. Let's play a game to help us tell the story.

Ask a child to be "It," and give him or her a rock. Set out the feathers, and have each child take one. Say: **We're going to play a game of Tag. The person holding the rock is It and** will try to tag as many of you as possible. It may not throw the rock or hit anyone with it. If you're tagged, you must freeze and stand still, but if someone touches you with a feather and says, "He is risen," you may run again. Whenever I say, "Roll the stone," some-one else can take a turn being It.

Play for five minutes. Then have children sit in a circle. Ask:

● How did it feel to be caught by It?

● How did you feel when someone freed you with the touch of a feather?

● How does Jesus' victory over death set us free?

Say: Jesus is risen! We celebrate because Jesus rose from the dead and he's alive today. Jesus has freed us from sin and death. That makes me happy! How about you? Let's gather the feathers and get ready for a special story.

2. EARTHQUAKE, ANGEL, STONE

Have kids sit in a circle. Give each child a small rock. Say: **I'll need your help to tell this story. First of all, can you make an earthquake?** Show children how to stamp their feet on the floor to make earthquake sounds. **That's great! When you hear the word "earthquake" in the story, you'll be ready. Now cover your eyes as though you're hiding from a bright light.** Let children practice shielding their eyes. **Great. Whenever you hear the word "angel," cover your eyes, because the Bible says the angels were bright like the sun. One last thing, can you gently roll your rock behind you when you hear the word "stone"?** Give children a moment to practice and then retrieve their rocks. **I think you're ready!**

> You'll need Bibles and a small rock for each child.

Read aloud the following story from Matthew 28:1-10. Pause after the italicized words to allow the children to respond.

Say: **In the morning of the first day of the week, Mary Magdalene and another woman named Mary went to look at the tomb. Suddenly there was a great *earthquake*. An *angel* came down from heaven. The *angel* went to the tomb and rolled the *stone* away. Then the *angel* sat down on the *stone*. He was shining as bright as light-ning. The soldiers who were guarding the tomb were so scared they shook with fear and fell down stiff like dead men!**

The *angel* said to the women, "Don't be afraid. I know you're looking for Jesus, who died on the cross. But he's not here. He has risen from death just like he said he would. Come and look where his body was. Then go quickly, and tell all his friends. Jesus will meet you all in Galilee.

The women left the *angel* and ran to tell Jesus' friends what had happened. Suddenly, Jesus met them and said "greetings." The women fell at his feet and worshiped him. He told them to go and tell his friends. The women were so happy! They ran as if they had *angels'* wings on their feet!

Ask:
- How do you think the women felt when they saw Jesus?
- How do you feel knowing that Jesus rose from the dead?
- Do you think Jesus' resurrection was the greatest miracle ever? Why or why not?

Say: **The Bible tells us that the women in this story were afraid but also very happy. I think they were probably surprised, too. Surprises can be exciting. Let's find out what it feels like to be surprised.**

EGGSTRA! EGGSTRA! 3.

You'll need a Bible and one colored egg for each child. Half of the eggs should be hard-boiled, and half should be uncooked and blown out. You'll also need newspapers and bowls.

Cover the floor or a table with newspaper. Form pairs. Have children sit in a circle around the papers or around the newspaper-covered table. Place bowls (one for every ten children) in the middle of the work area. Give each pair two colored eggs—one hard-boiled egg and one blown egg. Set the colored eggs in front of the children without allowing the children to touch them. Say: **I'm going to place two eggs in front of each pair. Please don't touch them until everyone has their eggs. Then you may take turns cracking open your eggs.**

After pairs break open their eggs, ask:
- What did you find inside?
- How were your two eggs different?
- How did you feel when you cracked open an empty egg?

Have a child read aloud Mark 16:1-3. Ask:
- What did the women expect to find when they reached the tomb?
- How would their feelings have differed if they had actually found Jesus in the tomb?

Say: **When you opened your eggs, you didn't expect some of them to be empty. In the same way, the tomb was supposed to have Jesus' body inside. The women didn't expect it to be empty.**

Have a child read aloud Mark 16:4-6. Ask:
- How do you think the women felt when they couldn't find Jesus?

Say: **The women were surprised and happy to know that Jesus had risen from death. And we're happy that Jesus is alive today. Let's use our eggshells to make something special that reminds us of the empty tomb.**

Have children place all the eggshells in piles in front of them. Put the peeled hard-boiled eggs in bowls, and refrigerate the eggs.

4. MOSAIC MASTERPIECES

Have children work in groups of four or five. Give each child a piece of poster board, and give each group eggshells and craft glue. Say: **Using the broken eggshells, make a mosaic to show how happy you are that Jesus is alive today. You may want to make a cross or a picture of the empty tomb, or you could even write "He is risen" with the colored eggshells. Use your imagination to celebrate the good news of the empty tomb.**

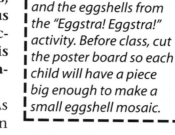

You'll need a Bible, poster board, craft glue, and the eggshells from the "Eggstra! Eggstra!" activity. Before class, cut the poster board so each child will have a piece big enough to make a small eggshell mosaic.

Give groups ten minutes to work on their mosaics. As they're working, read aloud Matthew 28:1-10. When groups have completed their mosaics, let them display and describe their masterpieces to the rest of the class.

Say: **When Jesus rose from the dead, everything changed. It's the most important event that ever happened in history! Because Jesus rose from the dead, we can have forgiveness for our sins. If we believe in Jesus, we can live forever with him in heaven. Take your mosaics home with you to show your families that you're happy Jesus is alive today. Tell them about God's forgiveness, the empty tomb, and how much Jesus loves us. For now, let's put the mosaics aside as we get ready to celebrate the Resurrection with music.**

5. SONRISE SONGS

Form groups of three. Give each group a section from the handout and pencils.

Say: **When people are happy, sometimes they like to sing. Sometimes they make up their own words to songs just for fun. Let's do that now to celebrate that Jesus is alive today. Work together in your groups to write a song using the words from the verse on your handouts.**

You'll need a Bible, pencils, a cassette recorder, a blank cassette tape, and photocopies of the "Sonrise Song" handout (p. 89). Before this activity, cut apart the Scripture references on the handout.

Encourage groups to look up and read their Scriptures, pick a familiar tune, and set their verses to music. Suggest simple tunes such as, "Frère Jacques," "Old MacDonald Had a Farm," or "Jesus Loves Me." Work with groups to help them with ideas. Give groups five to seven minutes to write their songs.

As children practice in their groups, allow one group at a time to go to another room to record its song on the blank cassette tape. Have an adult leader help groups make the recording. Once everyone has a song on tape, play all the songs for the entire group, and have kids guess who's singing. Then ask:

● **How do you think God feels when we sing to him?**

Say: **We're happy that Jesus is alive today. It's a good reason to sing and celebrate. We're going to keep on rejoicing with a special snack.**

You'll need a Bible, the hard-boiled eggs from the "Eggstra! Eggstra!" activity, plastic knives, mayonnaise, bread, a large mixing bowl, mixing spoons, paper plates, napkins, and a drink.

TEACHER TIP

Plan an alternate snack treat for children who don't like egg salad. Make sure it's comparable and not a sweet. Otherwise everyone will choose the alternative!

Before starting this activity, have children wash their hands. Form three groups. Have an adult helper available for each group. Say: **We're going to make egg-salad sandwiches to celebrate Jesus' resurrection. We'll need three groups: the Cutters, the Mixers, and the Spreaders. The Cutters will cut up the eggs on paper plates. The Mixers will add the mayonnaise and stir. The Spreaders will spread the egg salad on slices of bread. Then all of us will enjoy!**

Let groups work with adult help to complete their tasks. Make sure an adult helps the Cutters cut the eggs. Have the adult place the cut up eggs on paper plates. Let children pick up the plates and slide the eggs into the large bowl. Encourage the Mixers to take turns stirring the mixture. Have the adult leader add mayonnaise to taste. The Spreaders can use spoons to spread the egg salad on bread.

When all jobs are completed, say: **You've done a great job making these sandwiches. Now we can sit down and have an egg-salad celebration! First, listen as I read a verse.**

Read aloud Philippians 4:4. Then pray:

God, thank you for Easter morning. Because of Jesus rising from the dead, we're full of joy! Thanks for being with us now as we celebrate that Jesus is alive today!

Let everyone sit down to enjoy their egg-salad celebration.

Sonrise Song

Matthew 28:8-10

Luke 24:5-6

John 20:19-20

Psalm 9:1-2

Psalm 66:1-4

Colossians 3:1-2

The Great Commission

Scripture:
Matthew 28:16-20;
John 21:1-19

Good News:
We can spread the
good news about
Jesus to everyone.

Jesus had risen from the dead. All the disciples had seen him. But they weren't sure what to do next. As they walked on the beach and talked, some decided to go fishing. They worked hard all night, but caught nothing. Then, early in the morning as they neared land, a man called to them from shore and asked how the fishing had gone. He told them to cast their nets off the right side of their boat, so they did. The nets became so laden with fish that they couldn't be pulled into the boat. John motioned to Peter, indicating that the man on the shore was Jesus. Peter jumped in the water in his haste to get to shore. Jesus met with the disciples on the beach, and later told them what they should do next.

Like the disciples, children want to make God happy. Sometimes they just don't know how. Sharing Jesus' last words—the Great Commission—with children gives them a clear picture of what God wants them to do.

This lesson will help children realize that they can spread the good news about Jesus to everyone.

a look at the lesson

1. **DO YOU LOVE ME?** *(10 minutes)*
    Students will play a game of giggles when they ask each other "Do You Love Me?" and try not to laugh.

2. **STAND UP FOR JESUS** *(10 minutes)*
    Kids will stand while they listen to the story from John 21:1-14.

3. **SANDY FOOTPRINTS** *(10 minutes)*
    Children will make footprints from sand and listen to Psalm 119:105.

4. **SPREAD IT AROUND** *(10 minutes)*
    Kids will create "sandwiches" filled with ideas for telling their friends about Jesus.

5. **JESUS TAG** *(10 minutes)*
    Children will try to tell as many others as possible about Jesus before time is up.

6. **TAKE UP YOUR CROSS** *(10 minutes)*
    Kids will make crosses to help them spread the good news to friends.

preparation

Gather a Bible, newspapers, sandbox sand, shaker containers, glue sticks, poster board, markers, pencils, construction paper, and scissors. You'll also need photocopies of the "Spread It Around" handout (p. 96), brown twine, and twigs or chopsticks.

DO YOU LOVE ME?

You'll need a Bible.

Have children sit in a circle. Have a child read aloud John 21:15-19. Ask:

● **What did Jesus ask Peter?**
● **How many times did he ask him?**
● **How did that make Peter feel?**
● **Why do you think Jesus asked Peter the same question three times?**

Say: **Remember when Peter told people he didn't know Jesus? Do you remember how many times he did that? It was three times. Maybe Jesus wanted Peter to know that he was forgiven for those three times. We're going to play a game that will help us remember how much Jesus loves us. It's called Do You Love Me?**

Ask for a child to volunteer to be "It" first. Say: **It stays in the middle of the circle until someone laughs or giggles. When It comes to you and asks, "Do you love me?" three times, then you respond by saying, "Yes, I love you" three times also. But you must say it without smiling, giggling, or laughing. Let's try it.**

Select a new It each time someone laughs. Play until each child has had a turn to be It. Ask:

- How did it feel to ask if people loved you?
- Which was easier, to ask or to answer? Why?

Say: Jesus wanted Peter to know that he was forgiven. That's why he gave him three chances to answer, "Yes, I love you." Let's listen to what happened one day when the risen Jesus came to see his friends on the beach.

2. STAND UP FOR JESUS

Form two groups. Have groups sit in front of you, one group on your left and one on your right. Open the Bible to John 21:1-14, and show the kids the verses. Say: Today our story is from the book of John. While I'm reading the story, I want you to stand up for Jesus and Peter. The group on my left will stand whenever I say "Jesus." The group on my right will stand whenever I say "Peter." You'll remain standing until the other group stands up. Listen closely for the names.

You'll need a Bible.

Read aloud the following story from John 21:1-14. Pause at the italicized words to allow children to stand.

Say: One day *Peter* said, "I'm going to fish." Some of the disciples decided to go with him. They fished all night long but didn't catch anything. The next morning *Jesus* stood on the beach and called out to them, "Friends, did you catch anything?" *Peter* and the other disciples didn't know it was *Jesus*. They answered, "No."

Jesus told them to throw their net over the right side of the boat and then they would catch some. So *Peter* and the other disciples did what *Jesus* said and they caught so many fish that the net was stuck in the water, and they couldn't pull it back in the boat!

One of the disciples told *Peter*, "It's the Lord! It's *Jesus* on the beach!" *Peter* got so excited he jumped in the water to get to *Jesus*. *Jesus* had made breakfast for his friends. *Peter* and the other disciples were happy to see *Jesus* again. This was the third time they had seen him since he rose from the dead. *Peter* was happy that *Jesus* was alive! Ask:

- How do you think the disciples felt when they realized the man on the beach was Jesus?
- Why do you think Jesus made and ate breakfast with them?

Say: Jesus wanted his friends to know that he was alive. And he wanted them to keep living for him. He wanted them to spread the good news about him to everyone. He wanted them to follow him even when he wouldn't be here on earth. It was hard for them to understand then, and it's still hard for us today. How can we follow someone we can't see? Let's see if we can find some answers from the Bible.

You'll need a Bible, pencils, newspapers, sandbox sand, shaker containers, glue sticks, poster board, and markers. Cut the poster board into 8½-by-11-inch pieces. You'll need one piece for each child. Put the sandbox sand in shaker containers, such as empty baby powder containers. You may need to enlarge the holes depending on the coarseness of the sand.

Cover your work area with newspapers before beginning this activity. Say: **While we listen to verses that'll help us follow Jesus, we're going to make sandy footprints as reminders of how Jesus met with his friends on the beach.**

Give each child a piece of poster board and a pencil. Help children trace their feet on the poster board. It's easier to do one foot at a time starting with the left foot close to the left margin. Once the feet are traced with pencil, provide markers. Help children write the words from Psalm 119:105 at the top of their poster boards. Encourage the children to fill the foot area on their poster boards with glue.

Set out the shaker containers of sand, and have children shake the sand onto the glue. Be sure to keep the projects over the newspaper for easier cleanup.

When children have completed their footprints, have a volunteer read aloud Psalm 119:105. Ask:

● **What is our best guide for following Jesus?**
● **How can we learn more about what Jesus wants us to do?**

Say: **The Bible tells us how to follow Jesus. The more we read it, the more we know about what Jesus wants us to do. He's going to stay with us every sandy step of the way. And he's got work for us to do. We can spread the good news about Jesus to everyone! Let's find out how we can "spread" it around.**

SPREAD IT AROUND

You'll need a Bible, construction paper, scissors, markers, pencils, and one photocopy of the "Spread It Around" handout (p. 96) for each child.

Say: Jesus wants us to spread the good news about him. But how do we do that? Let's work together to think of ways we can tell our friends about Jesus.

Set out markers, construction paper, scissors, and pencils. Give each child a copy of the "Spread It Around" handout. Have children cut out their two slices of "bread." Then have them choose three colors of construction paper to cut into the same shapes by using the bread slices as patterns.

When everyone has finished, say: **Our sandwiches show the last words Jesus said while he was here on earth. He wanted his friends to spread the good news.** Ask:

● **What are some things you'd say to tell others about Jesus?**
● **Who can you tell about Jesus?**

Say: **Take the markers, and write some of the ideas we just talked about. Write your ideas on the construction paper "meat" and "cheese" you made for your sandwiches. If you want to write in yellow or red, you can pretend it's mustard or ketchup! Write at least one idea on** each of the three construction paper slices. Then put your sandwich together by placing one slice of bread, with words down, on the table. Next put your construction paper meat and cheese on top of that slice. Then place the second slice of bread so you can read the words. Pick up your sandwich, but don't take a bite! Save it to share with a friend!

Have kids set their sandwiches aside.

⑤ JESUS TAG

Ask a child to read aloud Mark 16:15.

Choose a child to be "It." Say: **We're going to play a different kind of Tag. It will still tag you just as in regular Tag, but then It will tell some good news about Jesus, such as, "Jesus loves us" or "He died for our sins." As soon as you've heard the good news, then you're It, too. Then you can tag others and tell them about Jesus. Each time you tag someone, you'll tell something good about Jesus.**

Let children play until everyone has heard about Jesus. Then have another child read aloud Mark 16:15.

Say: **Missionaries are people who go to different countries to tell others about Jesus. But did you know that we're all missionaries according to this verse? Amazing! Let's read it one more time to see.**

Have another child read aloud Mark 16:15. Ask:

● **Who's supposed to hear the good news?**
● **Who's supposed to be spreading it?**

Say: **We can spread the good news about Jesus to everyone. We're going to make crosses now that you can give to your friends as a way to share Jesus with them.**

> *You'll need a Bible. Plan to play this active game in an open room, or ask children to walk quickly or hop as they play, rather than running.*

⑥ TAKE UP YOUR CROSS

Say: To help you share Jesus, let's make wooden crosses to give as gifts.

Set out twigs, and have each child choose two. Show children how to put the twigs together in the shape of a cross. Then give each child a piece of twine. Help children wrap the twine around the twigs in a diagonal pattern. Then tie the strings off. Use the pattern in the margin as a guide.

Have children hold their crosses as they stand in a circle. Say: **Think of the person you'll give your cross to.**

Pray: **Dear Jesus, help us spread the good news about you to everyone. When we give away our crosses, help our friends know that you love them. In Jesus' name, amen.**

Have children take the crosses, sandwiches, and sandy footprints home.

> *You'll need a Bible, brown twine, and twigs or chopsticks. Before this activity, gather enough twigs or chopsticks so each child will have two. Cut a twelve-inch length of twine for each child.*

Spread It Around

"So go and make followers of all people in the world. Baptize them in the name of the Father and the Son and the Holy Spirit. Teach them to obey everything that I have taught you. You can be sure that I will be with you always, even until the end of this age" (Matthew 28:19-20).

"So go and make followers of all people in the world. Baptize them in the name of the Father and the Son and the Holy Spirit. Teach them to obey everything that I have taught you. You can be sure that I will be with you always, even until the end of this age" (Matthew 28:19-20).